THE MYSTIC TIE AND
THE WAY OF ONENESS

THE MASONIC CHART.

MASONRY'S MYSTICAL QUEST FOR UNITY,
WHOLENESS, AND HARMONY

C.R. DUNNING, JR.

Published By:

Stone Guild Publishing
P.O. Box 250167
Plano, TX 75025-0167
http://www.stoneguildpublishing.com/

First Paperback Edition Published 2024

ISBN-13 978-1-60532-111-0
ISBN- 1-60532-111-7

10 9 8 7 6 5 4 3 2 1

DEDICATION

THIS WORK IS COMMITTED TO THE GREAT MYSTERY AND LOVINGLY OFFERED TO ITS MANIFESTATION IN THE MYSTIC TIE.

"Dear brothers of the Mystic Tie!
You favored, enlightened few,
Companions of my social joy!"

– from "Farewell to the Brethren of St. James' Lodge,"
by Robert Burns

ACKNOWLEDGMENTS

Grateful recognition for inspiration, guidance, counsel, assistance, encouragement, friendship, and companionship is warmly extended to the following souls:

- John Miller and Jim Tresner, departed mentors

- Aaron Shoemaker and Baruti KMT-Sisouvong, admired contributors

- The brethren of the Allied Masonic Degrees, the Masonic Legacy Society, the Masonic Service Association of North America, and the Middle Chamber Program

- T∴F∴S∴, cherished consociate

- Matt Anthony, Ike Baker, Rudolf Berger, Shaun Bradshaw, Robert Davis, Pete Normand, Robert Sachs, Gordon Scheible, Ben Wallace, and Mohamad Yatim, respected manuscript reviewers

- Kevin and Lisa Main, esteemed publishers and editors

- Susan Dunning, beloved spouse

TABLE OF CONTENTS

FOREWORD
BY AARON SHOEMAKER, 33°

Past Sovereign Grand Master of the Grand Council of
Allied Masonic Degrees (USA)

Freemasonry has long captivated the imagination of many, draw-ing us in with its promises of mystery and personal growth. Before joining, many of us were intrigued by descriptions of Freemasonry we encountered through friends, movies, and books, which often em-phasized its secrecy. We wondered what Freemasonry taught and how it could help us grow. We may have heard strange expressions about the Craft, such as the "Mystic Tie" and the "Mysteries of Freemason-ry," which led us to search for something that seemed important yet elusive. Most of us, upon reflection after joining, if honest with our-selves, concluded that the meanings of these expressions and their relevance to our Masonic journey often remained unclear, even after being raised to the Sublime Degree of Master Mason. This foreword aims to introduce a unique new book that may guide both new initi-ates and seasoned Masons on a journey of deeper understanding and connection. As you read this book, I suggest you use it to help reflect upon your own journey, and that you consider how you might apply its practices to stoke your passion for the Craft.

Think back to your initiation and recall the moment when you first stood in the Lodge, surrounded by your new brothers. The solem-nity of the experience and the weight of the symbols presented likely inspired profound changes within you or at least ignited a desire to begin a personal quest. In your quest for deeper understanding, you might have joined numerous Masonic bodies, hoping each new degree would provide the insights you came seeking. You may have attended meetings, talks, and presentations, listened to podcasts, watched videos, and purchased countless books. Yet, articulating these experiences and the resulting personal growth to others has probably been challenging. Despite your significant investment of time, effort, and resources, the pursuit may sometimes have even felt fruitless. This book could help you make new breakthroughs.

My interest in Freemasonry began as a child when I noticed my grandfather wearing an unusual ring with a blue stone, some tools, and the letter G. I asked him about the ring, and he explained that the Masons were a group for "good men," and he promised to tell me more when the time came. Although he passed away before we could have that conversation, his influence, the example set by his integrity and the way that he lived, and the memory of that moment sparked a lifelong journey for me. This personal connection mirrors the experiences of many who are drawn to Freemasonry through family and friends. Over the years, I often recalled that conversation and grew more curious. Then, at 20, I overheard coworkers discussing Freemasonry. After some research and encouragement from my grandmother, I reached out to family and friends who were Masons. Their warm welcome and guidance led me to confidently petition the Fraternity.

Reflecting upon my journey, I realize that personal connections with friends and family who were Freemasons were a significant component in what inspired me to join the Craft. These relationships have kept me engaged in various Masonic activities, providing invaluable support and fellowship. They highlight the importance of fraternity in the Masonic experience. The sense of brotherhood, the satisfaction of working towards shared objectives, continuous personal development, and the joy of supporting others keep me deeply engaged. As we grow within the Craft, it is essential to recognize its impact on our lives and consider sharing our experience with friends and loved ones who might benefit from becoming Master Masons. Taking this step not only strengthens bonds, it can also enrich the Fraternity with new perspectives and experiences.

My journey took a deeper turn when I began to explore the history and symbolism of Freemasonry. This development led me to seek out personal practices that could enhance my understanding of the Craft's deeper meanings. It was during this quest that I met Brother Chuck Dunning.

In the early 2000s, I was introduced to Brother Chuck through a mutual friend. We were both in Oklahoma for a Masonic function and joined our friend at a brewery in Oklahoma City for an evening of conversation. While Brother Chuck and our friend were talking, the conversation turned toward meditation. As a young man and relatively new Mason, I was captivated by their discussion of meditating on Masonic symbols and concepts. They described a process where they could analyze these symbols almost as if they were suspended in time and space, allowing for limitless perspectives. I remember asking Chuck if this was truly possible, and he assured me that it was and that it was accessible to everyone.

Around that time, I began to travel for work to the area where Chuck lived. I reached out to him, and a series of visits soon followed during the evenings I was in town. These were pleasant visits where he and his wife typically prepared a nice meal, we enjoyed great conversation, and then Chuck and I would retreat to his study to discuss Freemasonry. It was during these discussions that Chuck introduced me to meditation and contemplative practice. He taught me how to focus on a single Masonic symbol, such as the Blazing Star, and visualize it in my mind's eye. Through this practice, I began to uncover layers of meaning and personal insight that were previously hidden. For example, meditating upon the Blazing Star helped me understand its representation of divine guidance and inner light, which became a source of inspiration in my daily life. Through these visits, I not only observed that Chuck was a true practitioner, but that he was able to teach others how to approach meditation and contemplative practice as well. Based on these experiences, I can confidently recommend Chuck and his writings about these subjects.

Freemasonry is often described as "a system of morality, veiled in allegory, and illustrated by symbols." Historically, there are various reasons why our teachings have been veiled, including societal and cultural factors. Additionally, we have always faced the challenge of communicating the insights and personal transformations that result from both the initiatic experience and the personal practice of meditating on our teachings and symbols. In his book *The Elements of Mysticism*, R.A. Gilbert highlights the challenge of conveying mystical experience, stressing the importance of developing a special language of both vocabulary and symbolism. Gilbert states there is significant difficulty

> *...in transmitting the experience to others in a meaningful way, for it is not an experience that is amenable to description or even interpretation in everyday language. The mystic may use the vocabulary of sense experience to describe the experience but the words must take on shades of meaning quite distinct from their ordinary use. (p. 89)*

This observation resonates deeply with my own journey in Freemasonry. Just as Gilbert describes, I found that ordinary language often fell short in expressing the profound insights gained through Masonic meditation. For instance, when I tried to explain the transformative power of the ritual to a non-Mason friend, I realized that only through the symbolic language of the Craft could I truly convey its impact.

In the pages that follow, Chuck addresses the many challenges outlined in this foreword. He provides a foundation for understanding the concepts by introducing a familiar vocabulary. This vocabulary is elaborated upon and enhanced through examples of experiential understanding via contemplative practice.

Engage with the practices that Brother Dunning introduces, and you can find that Freemasonry transforms into a profound way of being, rather than a set of rituals to simply be observed or performed. By incorporating these contemplative methods into your Masonic journey, you will uncover layers of meaning and personal insight that deepen your connection to the Craft and its teachings. This book is not just a guide; it is an invitation to explore the depths of Freemasonry and to experience the transformative power of its symbols and rituals in a new and meaningful way.

Aaron Shoemaker, 33°
Kansas City, MO
August 18, 2024

PREFACE

Dear Reader,

This is a book that almost wasn't. The manuscript was started after the publication of my second book, *The Contemplative Lodge* (2021), and prior to *A Rose Croix Oratory* (2023), but the inspiration for the latter took hold and became the priority. The manuscript for this text was set aside, and I was content to let it sit indefinitely, perhaps never to be completed and published. Then, one night in 2023, a couple of months after the previous book went public, I had a dream in which I was back at work on the manuscript. But, in my waking life, I was already beginning other creative projects, and I had the sense that time would unfold what I needed to understand, if anything, about the dream. A couple of weeks later, my family experienced a challenge that made it necessary to postpone or cancel many of my commitments and spend more time at home. As the necessity of that change became apparent, I recalled the dream and clearly understood that part of my time would be given to making this book a reality. So, if you find this work worthwhile, you can thank the mysterious author of that dream!

This preface provides initial considerations that should prove helpful to anyone proceeding through the book. First, please recognize the importance of clearly understanding how certain words are used herein; it may be advantageous to frequently consult the glossary. For now, we'll address the more particular meaning of *mysticism* as used in this text, and then we'll clarify what we do *not* include under the heading of mysticism. It also seems wise to touch on the perennial concern about Masonry distinguishing itself from religion and then consider some general preparatory comments about mystical pursuits. We will conclude with technical points about the book itself.

As used here, *mysticism* is about a human being *realizing union* with That which is regarded as most sacred, true or real, and which we represent with words like *God, the Creator, the Divine, the Monad, the One, the Absolute, Ultimate Reality, Love* (with a capital L), *Consciousness* (with a capital C), *the Ineffable, No-Thing*, or in Masonic language, the *Great Architect of the Universe*. From the perspective of this book, these terms are somewhat interchangeable, although each has noteworthy nuances. However, it must be clarified that within this text each name references a Great Mystery unlimited by all the concepts and sentiments such words and images stir within us. As distracting, misleading, and confusing as they can be, these symbols still have value in helping us open ourselves to mystical realization of our unity with that Mystery. So, please keep in mind that whenever this book uses language that seems to reduce the Great Mystery to some being or state (even *Great Mystery*), then you are encountering symbolism that reveals (literally "veils again") as well as conceals (literally "completely hides").

Many people consider mysticism to be an aspect of religion, and understandably so, since each of humanity's religions has its mystical elements. Indeed, each religion is arguably an outgrowth from at least one sage, prophet, or savior trying to communicate something from their own mystical realization. Mystics, philosophers, and religious scholars also find that the common elements of mystical awakening and insight across traditions point to an Absolute or Ultimate Reality that transcends religious differences, and I share their view and write from that perspective.[1] In this light, mystical awakening and realization is regarded as the experiential taproot of religion, not only as something that develops out of religion.

Throughout this book, the foundational philosophy on mysticism is Platonism, which means it is rooted in the works of the ancient Greek philosopher Plato and his followers such as Plotinus and Iamblichus. For many centuries, this philosophical school was the basis of how learned people understood the origin and manifestation of existence, including the nature and dynamics of the soul and its realization of greater truth, beauty, and goodness. There are many direct connections between Platonism and the ritual and symbolism of the Builder's Art. A few of those intersections are overtly explored, but many are left for discovery by those who are so inclined, which I strongly encourage. For now, maybe I can whet some appetites by noting that the Four Cardinal Virtues of the Entered Apprentice Degree and the Seven Liberal Arts of the Fellowcraft Degree were first presented to the world as complete sets by Plato in his book *Republic*. This philosophical context is also Masonically appropriate because over the millennia Platonism has shaped, and been interwoven with, the mystical movements of all the great Western religions. Thus, it is not limited by sectarianism and can therefore be potentially useful to the mystical realization of any brother.

The word *realization* should not be quickly passed over. In common parlance, it denotes becoming as aware as possible of something, having deeper insight and understanding about it, manifesting a potentiality, or fulfilling or accomplishing some intention or desire.

---

1. I acknowledge a perennialist orientation in my work, which becomes very evident as this text progresses. Perennialism holds that there is a single universal Truth, or Divine Source, or "an underlying basic shared human metaphysical reality," which gives rise to all pursuits of mystical transcendence, even though it is uniquely expressed in different cultural contexts. See Versluis, A. (2015). *Perennial Philosophy*. New Cultures Press.

It literally refers to a process of making something real (or more real) to oneself, which suggests that it is not merely conceptual but also experiential. All of the above applies to mystical realization. An additional facet for most of us is that mystical realization is a matter of ongoing development. Rather than arriving at some final achievement or completion, we work at more fully experiencing, comprehending, and infusing our lives with the truth of our union with Ultimate Reality, a truth geometrically represented by the circumpunct. Along the way, our realization may wax and wane from moment to moment, but overall, we aim for a more thorough and stable integration of it in all that we are and do.

Now we can further clarify what mysticism is *not* about, at least as it is more specifically understood in contemporary scholarship. It is not about developing psychic powers, doing divination, communicating with non-corporeal beings, or exploring metaphysical models of existence. Such things may be of interest to mystics, and they can even be included in the studies and practices of various mystical traditions, but they are not at the core of realizing union with the Divine. This book intends to focus on the indispensable elements of mysticism as found in a variety of traditions.

Given that mysticism is not limited to any particular religion, I believe it is appropriate for us to explore mystical concepts and practices together as Masons; this can be a very fitting and rewarding part of our traditional quest for Light. Indeed, some of the rites beyond the Craft Lodge encourage us to pursue such things. In doing so, each of us may choose to focus attention either strictly within the context of one's own religion, to proceed in consideration of many religious perspectives, or to try to ignore the mystical possibilities entirely. We are free to approach mysticism in Masonry the same way the Fraternity has traditionally dealt with issues of faith, salvation, prayer, symbolic representations of Deity, what we mean by words like *spirit* and *soul*, concepts of immortality, and the spiritual value of virtuous conduct and good works. In other words, we each make our own interpretations and choices and support the right of others to do the same. Thus, if pursuing a mystical quest through the Builder's Art, a Jewish Mason might arrive at a spiritual knowing akin to the Prophet Elijah's hearing of the "still small voice." A Christian Mason may receive an experiential understanding of what the Apostle Paul meant by "Christ in me." A direct encounter of the truth in the Prophet Muhammad's statement that "God is the Outward and the Inward" could be had by a Muslim Mason. Similar examples could be given for other religions, and those Masons in the increasingly common "spiritual but not religious" category might realize integration with the Supreme Archetype or awaken to Pure Consciousness. The realization of any Mason might also go beyond such terms in ways that cannot be captured in words or images.

This text's use of the term *oneness* also warrants explanation. It is, of course, synonymous with *unity*. Thus, in one sense it refers to the indivisibility of something. In another, it refers to connectedness between seemingly different things. In yet another, it refers to the Divine, in which case it would be appropriate to give it an initial capitalization – *Oneness* is the nature of the One, it is Ultimate Reality. However, in the context of mystical considerations, these different meanings of *oneness* can be so fluid and interpenetrating that something could be lost by trying to make a distinction with the presence or absence of the capital O. Therefore, throughout this book the lowercase o is used, and readers are encouraged to be aware of its various implications.

While the present intentions are to provide reflections on mystical concepts and practices relevant to the Builder's Art, this book does not provide a thorough academic or comparative treatment of either the historical, theoretical, or technical aspects of mysticism. What is offered here is grounded in my own experience and understanding of contemplative practices and mystical states of consciousness, and how I see them pertaining to Masonry. It is my firmly held view that our words about mysticism are best rooted in actual practice. Therefore, while scholarly studies of mysticism are important, I urge sincere aspirants to be more concerned with practical engagement of a contemplative path than with gathering, comparing, and contrasting other peoples' ideas and insights about mysticism, which certainly includes mine.

With the clear emphasis placed on practice, there are some comments I want to make about preparation for such work. To begin with, it is taken for granted that readers already are Masons or are seriously interested in Masonry, and thus have some familiarity with the Builder's Art. I build upon that assumption to make the case for a mystical perspective within our tradition. Mystics across traditions, and now scientists studying mysticism and contemplative practice, have observed that harmful consequences can arise from mystical aspirations being pursued outside the context of a well-established wisdom tradition that includes development of moral virtues and psychological wellbeing. The Craft is such a tradition, and those who sincerely engage its teachings can indeed experience the kind of character development supportive of genuine mystical realization.

Next, it is important to appreciate the integrated nature of any systematic approach to mystical contemplation, understanding that the various practices are not only supportive of each other, but are also provided as an integrated whole. This book attempts to provide guidance for a sufficiently comprehensive approach within the Masonic tradition, while leaving plenty of leeway for self-directed study and practice. However one proceeds, consistently productive contemplative practice requires sustained commitment to even the most fundamental methods, and often long past the time when they have lost their novelty and entertainment value. There are no shortcuts or substitutes for the ego-challenging and capacity-building discipline required by a genuine path of inner work; it is not a casual pastime or a hobby to be merely tinkered with. To enter such a quest is one meaning of the word *initiation* and the ceremonial process we call "initiation" is weakened without it, but its significance can also get distorted and become deceiving. Precautionary considerations are therefore in order.

There are countless descriptions of mystical initiations and the ensuing spiritual quests that include hopeful visions of integration, ascension, liberation, transcendence, and illumination. This book also urges its readers to consider the desirable transformations that mystical practices can facilitate. The best intention behind such words is to inspire and motivate, but it can be easy for them to become the basis of narcissistic dreams of beatific sanctification, unshakable inner peace, untarnished virtue, profound wisdom, perfect clarity, and even superhuman magical powers. Indeed, some sources explicitly evoke such extremes. However, speaking from my own firsthand experience, and the experience of working with many other individuals, this kind of *spiritual glamor* can be quite misleading and harmful.

Spiritual glamor has lots of shortcomings. For one thing, it too easily urges a focus on the supposed outcomes rather than the process of an initiatic mystical quest. By *process*, I mean the inner work of deep exploration, honest assessment, disciplined adjustment, and intentional actualization of the deepest potentials within oneself. Without giving time and energy to those things, it is very easy to slip into the illusion that the vision of mystical realization is being attained simply by espousing it fervently enough and associating with others who do likewise, which is basically the same as many people's ordinary religious and political lives.

Another problem with a focus on outcomes is that it assumes an initiatic system, such as the degrees of Masonry, is just a recipe to follow for cooking up the kind of person one wishes to be. The errors here are (a) failing to recognize that following a spiritual path is a developmental process, which is to say it changes a person in ways that elicit further changes, and (b) failing to understand that the person one is at a given moment may be poorly prepared to accurately anticipate exactly what will change or the precise effects those changes will have on one's values, beliefs, and priorities. As an analogy, consider how few of us at 13 years of age could have sufficiently predicted who we would be at 30. Also reflect on the fact that most college students change their majors at least once, and that a significant percentage of college graduates end up in careers not directly related to their bachelor's degrees. These issues cannot be simply ascribed to poor decision-making. Rather, they reveal our need to continually rediscover and reinvent ourselves as we adjust to the mysterious, complex, and unpredictable demands of ordinary life. It should be no surprise that similar challenges arise on initiatic quests leading us even deeper into life's mysteries.

Aside from a focus on outcomes, another problem with spiritual glamor is that it can set one up for destructive negativity when its illusions are shattered. I have watched myself and others be overcome with pain, rage, despair, anxiety, shame, regret, cynicism, and even paranoia when the spiritual glamor evaporated. Worse yet, I have seen myself and others double-down on the spiritual glamor, desperately trying to regress into the naïve bliss of something that should be outgrown, and thus willfully creating a spiritual dissonance hidden deep within the shadows of the soul, sometimes festering in secret guilt and shame for false faithfulness.

One of the fascinating things about inner work is that it can accelerate the shattering of spiritual glamor. When one is attentively turned inward, it can be harder to ignore and deny unpleasant truths, doubts, or uncertainties about life and oneself. Furthermore, when one's practice includes contemplation and implementation of virtues, mental exercises, and other forms of self-discipline, weaknesses and shortcomings are bound to be noticed. An honest assessment of such things makes it clear that one's path is often anything but a pleasant stroll leading to a celebratory welcome into a heavenly garden of bliss.

In contrast to the relative violence of disillusionment forced by the abrupt emergence of unwelcome truth, inner work provides the opportunity to knowingly and willingly open the door for change. In fact, this opening is an essential element of authentic initiation, which also includes at least symbolic acknowledgments of the mystery and hard work involved in facilitating significant change. When initiation and inner work are understood this way, one naturally enters upon them with some degree of trepidation. Even so, there is still a driving sense of wonder, adventure, and willingness to take the risks that carry one forward. One engages the quest expecting the unexpected as a necessary and desirable factor for real transformation, and thus shattering of spiritual glamor is less likely to be traumatic.

For anyone who is interested in taking up such a quest, it is important to remain mindful that one cannot predict exactly who or what one will become along the way. Of course, some general ideas, hopes, and aspirations can be quite helpful, but the extent to which we are unwilling to become different from who we are, or from who we *fantasize about being*, is the extent to which we erect barriers to authentic learning, growth, and transformation. Deep down we all know that change happens whether we engage it voluntarily or not, and it can do so with very little regard for how we would prefer it to happen or where we would want it to lead.

I have found the effects of initiation and inner work leading me and others through noteworthy departures from previously held beliefs and understandings of the world and ourselves. They have led to changes in our religion, politics, relationships, pastimes, and careers, many of which would not have been desired or approved by previous versions of ourselves. Furthermore, such changes have often been later supplanted by yet others, so that at times they have seemed more like points in pendulum swings or spirals than steps on any linear course. On a quest like this, one never has a final destination. It is instead an ever-evolving process of growth, and it can be truly astounding and filled with wonder, but often not quite as glamorous as we might prefer.

Love is the secret fire making it possible for one to repeatedly seek, welcome, and work through such challenges. And here is a *very important point* to keep in mind while reading and reflecting on this book: Love as it is spoken of here is the manifestation of Divine Love, mysteriously transcending the dualities and oppositions in which we typically try to confine it. It is not only in the bright, warm, pleasant, comforting things we commonly prefer to identify with the word *love*, but can also be found in the dark, cold, unpleasant, and disturbing aspects of life. After all, it is love that causes a parent to forcefully yank a child back from the path of an oncoming car, even though the parent feels it as a fearful act, and for the child, it may be experienced as shocking violence. On the mystical quest, Love is not only the driving force that can break through all obstacles, but it is also the essence of what we are seeking and the light that illuminates the path. One way I came to understand the connection between love and the shattering of spiritual glamor is expressed in this poem:

LET LOVE BREAK YOU

Seeker of the ultimate truth,

Pursuer of the highest wisdom,

Yearner for God,

If you don't let love break you,

You won't find what you want.

If love doesn't swallow

Every one of your desires,

Doesn't hang your soul on a cross,

Dissolve your mind,

Burst your heart open wide,

Burn away every inch of your flesh,

And grind your bones to nothingness,

And if that isn't your choice,

Over and over again,

Then you will only be playing

A game of hide and seek

With the phantom you call "me."

Now, I wish to make some technical notes about this book. I begin by declaring that it is offered in service to the Craft, and for that reason my royalties are going to Masonic philanthropies. You are doing good for others by making a retail purchase of a new copy.

This work is largely a compilation of lecture notes and material borrowed from my own published articles and blog posts, all pasted together with some new writing; it may therefore seem a bit rough around the edges. Readers will not often find the detailed citations fitting for a more scholarly text, and some quotations are longer than is considered good form by today's standards. Because these pieces were not originally written as parts of a single text, some of the arguments and even specific wording may be repeated from one section to another. I ask you to regard such repetition as emphasis on the significance I have found in those points.

Here are two notices I feel ethically moved to make: First, I affirm that no individual or organization speaks for all of Masonry; the views offered in this book are solely my own unless otherwise noted. Second, unless otherwise stated, ritual and monitorial references are from the Preston/Webb varieties of the Craft or Blue Lodge degrees and from the Southern Jurisdiction in the USA for the Scottish Rite degrees.

Finally, my hope is that this book offers inspiration, encouragement, and useful instructions for Masons with mystical and contemplative inclinations. The offered insights might be intriguing or entertaining, but their greatest value is only found in conjunction with actual practices like mindfulness, meditation, dreamwork, dialog, and virtue. If nothing else, maybe this text can stir motivation to take up such practices for readers who have not already done so. In the process, some might have the sense that they are rediscovering things that, deep down inside, they already knew.

To wrap up this preface, I offer another poem.

OUR MYSTIC QUEST

The brightest light the soul might know

Is never to be seen.

The sweetest fruits one's life can grow

Hang from a hidden tree.

The truest words that we may speak

Are not formed by the tongue.

The greatest goals that we would seek

Are never to be won.

The surest path of wisdom's way

Cannot be trod by feet.

The purest prayer that one may pray

Will never be complete.

Our mystic quest pursues the One

No mind can hope to hold,

But with a flame bright as the sun

Our hearts are ever bold.

Our union with the Most Divine

Is not found high above.

In silent depths it waits reclined

To welcome all in love.

In Love's embrace we are at home

Though easily forget,

That all beneath the heavens' dome

Is filled with Heaven yet.

Yours in the Mystic Tie,
Chuck Dunning

CHAPTER ONE
THE MYSTIC TIE AND SPIRITUAL UNION

The phrase *Mystic Tie* may well have been invented by our poet brother, Robert Burns, when he penned these lines at the beginning of his "Farewell to the Brethren of St. James' Lodge" in 1786:

> *Adieu! a heart-warm fond adieu;*
> *Dear brothers of the mystic tie!*
> *Ye favoured, enlighten'd few,*
> *Companions of my social joy*

Whatever depths Burns might have personally found in those two words, they have become a popular symbol in Masonic tradition. As such, they are open to further investigation and deeper contemplation. So, is the Mystic Tie simply our feelings of brotherly affection and the obligations we vow to each other? Surely it is at least these, but we shall see that it can mean much more.

Exploring meanings for the Mystic Tie, the Masonic Service Association's *Short Talk Bulletin* of October 1940 notes that part of it is our ritual:

> *...this golden chain of sounds which die even as they are born, and yet which never cease sounding once they have been taken into the heart—they are a part of the Mystic Tie.*

It then goes on to add:

> *Friendship is a part of the Mystic Tie; that glory of life in which a man finds a man in whom he can trust, for whom he would labor, with whom he would live. Not the greatest poet who has yet lived has been able to define friendship. We know what it is, but we cannot explain it. Yet it is there, alive, vital, a part of Lodge life, an integer in the whole, and so a part of the Mystic Tie.*

The inscrutability of the nature of friendship leads to this recognition about the Mystic Tie:

> *Mystery is a part of it—indeed, is it not named for mystery? And Freemasonry is so filled with mysteries! From whence came it, this chain of fraternity which began we know not when and grew we know not how? And whither does it go? The one as much a mystery as the other.*

In further reflection on the mystery of the Mystic Tie, the article says:

> *None who have known it would think of denying the strength*
> *of the Mystic Tie. None who have its cord about their hearts*
> *would loose it. None can wholly comprehend it: none define,*
> *describe it. It exists; it works its gentle miracles: it is as mighty*
> *as it is intangible.*

Finally, the *Short Talk Bulletin* ends its contemplation on the Mystic Tie with a poem by Brother Carl Claudy, "The Road."

> *So many men before thy Altars kneel*
> *Unthinkingly, to promise brotherhood;*
> *So few remain, humbly to kiss thy rood*
> *With ears undeafened to thy mute appeal;*
> *So many find thy symbols less than real,*
> *Thy teachings mystic, hard to understand;*
> *So few there are, in all thy far flung band*
> *To hold thy banner high and draw thy steel*
> *And yet ... immortal and most mighty, thou!*
> *What hath thy lore of life to let it live?*
> *What is the vital spark, hid in thy vow?*
> *Thy millions learned as thy dear paths they trod,*
> *The secret of the strength thou hast to give:*
> *"I am a way of common men to God."*

These references highlight that *mystic* evokes the "hard to understand" quality of mystery. In this context, the poem ponders a "vital spark" and "secret strength" in Masonry, and that question is answered by asserting that the Craft is *a way to God*. This response is quite fitting, since *mystic* refers not merely to mystery in a general sense, but more specifically to *spiritual* mysteries. Thus, the Mystic Tie is not reducible to sentiments of affection or feelings of interpersonal connectedness and commitment. Rather, it is a Divine mystery that inspires such attitudes.

To better understand the implications of the Mystic Tie, let us look closer at the term *mystic*. Its origin is Greek, where the root word means "to close" or "to conceal." Thus, *mystes* was the title of an initiate in the ancient Greek mystery religions where hidden truths of life and the cosmos were dramatically revealed. Perhaps because of the ecstatic experiences induced within their rites, the term *mysticism* eventually became most broadly associated with any practices or beliefs pertaining to non-ordinary states of consciousness. However, in modern comparative religious studies, mysticism is more specifically about *direct experience of Ultimate Reality*, while conceptualizations and expressions of Ultimate Reality are understood to vary according to culture, religion, and individual abilities. As the most relevant case in point, within the Abrahamic religions from which Masonry arose, an experience of Ultimate Reality is traditionally described as "union with God," and mystics are those persons who contemplate, seek, or open themselves to a state, knowledge, or realization of such union.

In Middle Eastern monotheism, evidence of a long-held awareness of God's oneness with each of us and all creation is easy enough to find. Consider these examples:

JUDAISM

> *Then God said, "Let us make human beings so that they are like us." [...] So God created human beings in his own likeness. He created them to be like himself. [...] Then the Lord God formed a man. He made him out of the dust of the ground. God breathed the breath of life into him. And the man became a living person. (Genesis 1:26-27, 2:7)*

I am the Lord, and there is none else. I form the light, and create darkness: I make peace, and create evil: I the Lord do all these things. (Isaiah 45:6-7)

This is what the Lord says: "Heaven is my throne, and the earth is my footstool. Where is the house you will build for me? Where will my resting place be? Has not my hand made all these things, and so they came into being?" (Isaiah 66:1-2a)

CHRISTIANITY

In the beginning was the Word, and the Word was with God, and the Word was God. The same was in the beginning with God. All things were made by him; and without him was not anything made that was made. In him was life; and the life was the light of men. (John 1:1-4)

I am praying not only for these disciples but also for all who will ever believe in me through their message. I pray that they will all be one, just as you and I are one—as you are in me, Father, and I am in you. And may they be in us so that the world will believe you sent me. I have given them the glory you gave me, so they may be one as we are one. I am in them and you are in me. May they experience such perfect unity that the world will know that you sent me and that you love them as much as you love me. Father, I want these whom you have given me to be with me where I am. (John 17:20-23)

He is the God who made the world. He also made everything in it. He is the Lord of heaven and earth. [...] God did this so that people would seek him. And perhaps they would reach out for him and find him. They would find him even though he is not far from any of us. "In him we live and move and exist." As some of your own poets have also said, "We are his children." (Acts 17:24-28)

ISLAM

The East and the West belong to God. Whichever way you turn, there is the Face of God. God is all pervading and all knowing. (Surah 2, Ayah al-Baqarah, verse 115)

Do you not see that God is glorified by all those in the heavens and the earth, even the birds as they soar? Each instinctively knows their manner of prayer and glorification. And God has perfect knowledge of all they do. To God alone belongs the kingdom of the heavens and the earth. And to God is the final return. (Surah 24, An-Nur, verses 41-42)

BAHA'I

After passing through the Valley of Knowledge, which is the last plane of limitation, the wayfarer cometh to the Valley of Unity and drinketh from the cup of the Absolute, and gazeth on the Manifestations of Oneness. In this station he pierceth the veils of plurality, fleeth from the worlds of the flesh, and ascendeth into the heaven of singleness. With the ear of God he heareth, with the eye of God he beholdeth the mysteries of divine creation. (The Seven Valleys and the Four Valleys, p. 18)

So, we can now see more clearly what the *Short Talk Bulletin* on the Mystic Tie intends by concluding with Claudy's description of the Craft as a way to God. It suggests that the various aspects of our shared fraternal experience, and the bonds we aim to establish and improve through them, are rooted in, inspired by, and reflections of union with God. In short, the word *tie* expresses union, and *mystic* clarifies that it is of a divine nature.

Thus, in its grandest sense, the phrase *Mystic Tie* expresses the mysterious oneness of the incomprehensible All with the ineffable One. The followers of our friend and brother Pythagoras represented this unity of creation and its Creator with the circumpunct, a point within a circle, which has an important place in the Builder's Art. Consider the following words from Sickel's *General Ahiman Rezon* (1871), reflecting on the Pythagorean interpretation of the circumpunct.

> *The number ONE was the Point within the Circle, and denoted the central fire, or GOD; because it is the beginning and ending—the first and the last. It signified, also, love, concord, piety, and friendship; because it is so connected that it cannot be divided into parts.*

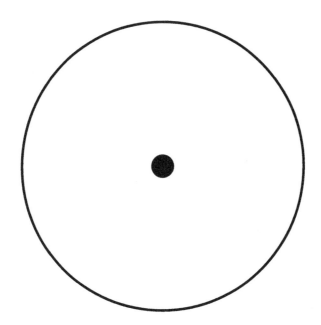

Those words speak not only to the cosmological significance of the circumpunct but also to its social meaning, and thus to its representation of the meanings we are exploring within the phrase *Mystic Tie*. The idea that human beings can realize the Mystic Tie – the indissoluble bond with Deity, each other, and all – is also not unique to Masonry's monotheistic background. Indeed, what we now propose as this more complete understanding of the Craft's Mystic Tie can be found across a wide variety of spiritual traditions. For example:

NAVAJO

Hozhoni, hozhoni, hozhoni [2]
Hozhoni, hozhoni, hozhoni.
The Earth, its life am I, hozhoni, hozhoni
The Earth, its feet are my feet, hozhoni, hozhoni
The Earth, its legs are my legs, hozhoni, hozhoni
The Earth, its body is my body, hozhoni, hozhoni
The Earth, its thoughts are my thoughts, hozhoni, hozhoni
The Earth, its speech is my speech, hozhoni, hozhoni
The Earth, its down-feathers are my down-feathers, hozhoni, hozhoni.

The sky, its life am I, hozhoni, hozhoni.
The mountains, their life am I, hozhoni, hozhoni.
Rain-mountain, its life am I, hozhoni, hozhoni.
Changing-Woman, her life am I, hozhoni, hozhoni.
The Sun, its life am I, hozhoni, hozhoni.
Talking God, his life am I, hozhoni, hozhoni.
House God, his life am I, hozhoni, hozhoni.
White corn, its life am I, hozhoni, hozhoni.
Yellow corn, its life am I, hozhoni, hozhoni.
Corn-pollen, its life am I, hozhoni, hozhoni.
The corn-beetle, its life am I, hozhoni, hozhoni.
Hozhoni, hozhoni, hozhoni
Hozhoni, hozhoni, hozhoni.
("Song of Creating People," also known as "Its Life Am I")

---

2. *Hozhoni* means beauty, harmony, and peace.

HINDUISM

*This is the teaching of Uddalaka to Shvetaketu, his son; [...]
So, through spiritual wisdom, dear one, we come to know that
all life is one. In the beginning was only Being, one without a
second. Out of himself he brought forth the cosmos and entered
into everything in it. There is nothing that does not come from
him. Of everything he is the inmost Self. He is the truth; he
is the Self Supreme. You are that, Shvetaketu; you are that.
(Chandagyoga Upanishad)*

BUDDHISM

*Do not err in this matter of self and other. Everything is
Buddha without exception. Here is that immaculate and final
stage, where thought is pure in its true nature. The fair tree
of thought that knows no duality, spreads through the triple
world. It bears the flower and fruit of Compassion, and its
name is service of others. (Saraha)*

TAOISM

*Master Tung-kuo asked Chuang Tzu, "This thing called the
Way—where does it exist?"*

Chuang Tzu said, "There's no place it does not exist."

"Come," said Master Tung-kuo, "you must be more specific!"

"It is in the ant."

"As low a thing as that?"

"It is in the panicgrass."

"But that is lower still!"

"It is in the tiles and shards."

"How can it be so low?"

"It is in the piss and dung."

(Chuang Tzu)

NEOPLATONISM

> *The [Divine] Soul gives itself to every point in this vast body
> [of creation], and vouchsafes its being to every part, great and
> small, though these parts are divided in space and manner of
> disposition, and though some are opposed to each other, others
> dependent on each other. But the Soul is not divided, nor does
> it split up in order to give life to each individual. All things
> live by the Soul **in its entirety**; it is all present everywhere.
> The heaven, vast and various as it is, is one by the power of the
> Soul, and by it is this universe of ours Divine. The sun too is
> Divine, and so are the stars; and we ourselves, if we are worth
> anything, are so on account of the Soul. (Plotinus)*

Before we move on from consideration of Claudy's wonder-
fully poignant poem, we should note that its final words assert that
Masonry offers a mystic way of oneness to "common men." That
observation is significant because, as Andrew Harvey has written in *The
Essential Mystics: The Soul's Journey into Truth* (1998),

> *The word **mystic** may mislead or intimidate some people – the
> prestige accorded to it has traditionally been so exalted that
> they feel such heightened perception and joy belong to and are
> attainable by only a few chosen human beings. This is far from
> the case. Mystical experience is always available – like the di-
> vine grace it is – to any who really want it; and all human be-
> ings are given in the course of their lives glimpses into the heart
> of the real which they are free to pursue or forget.*

The Builder's Art offers an alternative to ways of encountering
the Great Mystery that have typically seemed accessible only to the
most elite ranks of erudite philosophers, devout monks, or world-
renouncing hermits. Masonry can be a mystical quest for ordinary
people leading ordinary lives, and yet it has the potential to bring them
to extraordinary experiences, understandings, and realizations. This

view of the Craft as a way of communion with Deity is not a rare oddity in philosophical perspectives on Masonry, as evidenced by the following statements:

> *This union is symbolized by the familiar conjunction of the square and the compasses. The square is the emblem of the soul; the compasses of the Spirit which indwells in that soul. At first the Mason sees the points of the compasses concealed behind the square, and, as he progresses, their points emerge from that concealment until both become superimposed upon the square. Thus is indicated the progressive subordination of the soul and the corresponding coming forward of the ultimate Spirit into personal consciousness, so that the Mason can "work with both those points," thus becoming an efficient builder in the spirit and rendering the circle of his own being complete by attaining conscious alliance with his ultimate and only true self. (W.L. Wilmshurst, The Masonic Initiation)*

> *When properly applied to a person's life, toleration and love of others develop, creating a true feeling of brotherhood and a oneness with God. (Samuel L. Cochran, "Hidden Masonic Lessons," Virginia Research Lodge No. 1777)*

> *The Freemason will only find his goal when his perception passes through the visible order and he is raised to the spiritual reality which exists at its heart: the link and key to which lies in his own heart, which, as he learns in the First Degree, must first be true, and then thus, the mason is centred and may partake in the divine presence concentrated therein. Thus, while in the physical realm he is in harmony with the spiritual law behind the visible universe: he is at one with the Great Architect's design. [...] When the mason achieves mystic union with God (in an allegorical sense), the light-darkness duality (the chequered floor) disappears. The union can no longer be described. (Giuliano Di Bernardo, Past Grand Master of the Grand Lodge of Italy, "Enlightenment from the Ritual")*

In Freemasonry the lost word has become a symbol of the never-ending search for light, or truth, which is another way to say the search for unity or oneness with God. (Grand Lodge of Ohio, "Master Mason Education Script")

When we find Masonry identified as to its source with God, the reference, however unconscious, is to that original and positive knowledge with which the mystics have endowed the archetypal man when he was first differentiated from Deity, but still enjoyed the immersion of his individual soul in the divine consciousness, and thus knew all things in God. From this point of view the Masonic object of research, mystically interpreted, would be, for such speculations, simply this primeval knowledge, and the system embodied by Masonry would be a process for its recovery. (Arthur Edward Waite, Studies in Mysticism)

...the mature mason has learned through the craft that man is, without any doubt whatever, an Eternal Being; an Eternal Being burdened with mortality, wending a torturous path through that mortality to a reward beyond his comprehension – a union with God. (J.S. Woods, "The Man in Masonry: The Character of a Mature Mason")

*The [Masonic] link to the kabbalistic tradition becomes more evident when the initiatory aspect of the [Hiramic] legend is emphasized. At the core of the Jewish Kabbalah lies the fundamental aim of the individual experience of the Godhead, or **Unio Mystica**. It is this fundamental aim that links the two traditions together in a **functional manner**. Both traditions focus on a direct identification with, or experience of, the Godhead. (Henrick Bogdan and J.A.M. Snoek, Handbook of Freemasonry)*

The goal of both sciences [Kabbalah and Freemasonry] is the same, that the entire mankind becomes better, ultimately perfect, to realize the ultimate plan of creation and unite with God. (Nebojsa Nikolic, Kabbalah and Freemasonry: Becoming One with God)

If we dissect Freemasonry we will find [...] a Quest for something that has been lost [...] passing through a regular series of what may be called Expansions of Consciousness [...] towards union with God [...] Man himself, being "made in the image of God," is therefore [...] capable, through the development of full knowledge of himself as such, of Union with God. (Rev. J.K. Cleland, "The Masonic Trinity and the Way of the Cross," Dormer Masonic Study Circle)

This Royal Secret [of Scottish Rite Freemasonry], or equilibrium, prepares us to understand the Holy Doctrine. This Doctrine, simply stated, is that the human spirit is a ray of the Divine Light. As it was written in the Psalms, all of you are children of the Most High. Thus, God dwells in the human soul, and the divine intermingles with the human. God is near at hand with His creatures, not afar off and inaccessible, but embracing all with His love. The wise and good of all ages and religions have been close to God and His Kingdom of Heaven. Therefore, the Holy Doctrine everywhere taught that the soul could be enlightened and invigorated and made to resemble God, whose image it is. By this, the faithful are at last to unite again with Him of whom they are an emanation. (Scottish Rite Ritual Monitor & Guide)

CONFRONTING THE ILLUSION OF SEPARATION

I believe that God is everything and God is everywhere. There is no separation between God and us. [...] Thus in the great light of God, we are shards, fragments, waves, or particles of that very same stuff. The separation we feel, the isolation that leads to desperation, that creates big and small, strong and weak egos, that makes us do horrible as well as exquisite things to each other and all that is around us that is God as well – is illusory.[3]

One of the most common mystical insights shared among spiritual people of all times, an insight now affirmed by physicists, is that our notion of absolute separateness is an illusion. Instead, our deepest thinkers and clearest seers insist that we are all one, that everything in existence is intimately interconnected in countless ways, and that we share in a common essence. The use of the term *illusion* in this context is not meant to be merely dismissive, as if to say the experience of separateness may be discounted as trivial or meaningless. Neither should those whose awareness is entirely bound within this illusion be regarded with indifference, disdain, or prideful pity. It is a powerful, pervasive, and persistent misperception of reality that is quite understandable for many reasons. Even mystics who have known transcendent experiences of unity must still manage this illusion; it is seemingly woven into the fabric of human existence.

To give the matter further contemplation, consider the following quotes, taken from a variety of individuals representing different traditions and areas of expertise.

A human being is a part of the whole called by us "the universe," a part limited in time and space. He experiences himself, his thoughts and feelings, as something separate from the rest – a kind of optical illusion of consciousness. This delusion is a kind of prison for us, restricting us to our personal desires and affection for a few persons nearest to us. Our task must be to free ourselves from this prison by widening the circle of understanding and compassion to embrace all living creatures and the whole of nature in its beauty. (Albert Einstein)

3. Sachs, Robert, (2016). *The Ecology of Oneness: Awakening in a Free World*, 76-77. iUniverse. Note that Robert Sachs is a Freemason.

We are here to awaken from our illusion of separateness. [...] Human beings are not separate from each other or Nature. We are totally interrelated and our actions have consequences to all. What we do to others we do to ourselves. What we do to the Earth we do to ourselves. (Thich Nhat Hanh)

Identification with your mind creates an opaque screen of concepts, labels, images, words, judgments, and definitions that blocks all true relationship. It comes between you and yourself, between you and your fellow man and woman, between you and nature, between you and God. It is this screen of thought that creates the illusion of separateness, the illusion that there is you and a totally separate "other." You then forget the essential fact that, underneath the level of physical appearances and separate forms, you are one with all that is. (Eckhart Tolle)

The first peace, which is the most important, is that which comes within the souls of people when they realize their relationship, their oneness with the universe and all its powers, and when they realize that at the center of the universe dwells the Great Spirit, and that this center is really everywhere, it is within each of us. (Black Elk)

Whatever affects one directly, affects all indirectly. I can never be what I ought to be until you are what you ought to be. This is the interrelated structure of reality. (Martin Luther King, Jr.)

All differences in this world are of degree, and not of kind, because oneness is the secret of everything. (Swami Vivekananda)

The God who existed before any religion counts on you to make the oneness of the human family known and celebrated. (Desmond Tutu)

The fundamental delusion of humanity is to suppose that I am here and you are out there. (Yasutani Roshi)

*The whole idea of compassion is based on a keen awareness of
the interdependence of all these living beings, which are all
part of one another, and all involved in one another. (Thomas
Merton)*

*Wisdom is nothing but a preparation of the soul, a capacity, a
secret art of thinking, feeling and breathing thoughts of unity
at every moment of life. (Herman Hesse)*

Different authorities and traditions offer different explanations
for how the illusion of separation arises. For now, we reference the
Book of Genesis because it has such a prominent place in the ritual
of most Masonic jurisdictions and because its myth of creation and
the subsequent Fall of Humanity is familiar to most Masons. As we
do so, it is recommended that you try to not be too literal about the
myth's temporal language, its reference to a past unfolding of events for
persons no longer alive. Rather, consider that it describes processes that
are always ongoing.

The first word in Genesis is the Hebrew *bereshith*, commonly
translated as "in the beginning." Many mystics and theologians find
it significant that the first word on the first act of God starts with the
second letter of the Hebrew alphabet. This fact is taken as a hint of
THAT which is uncreated, which pre-exists creation, represented by
the first Hebrew letter, *aleph*. Thus, beyond the beginning, unlimited
by time and space, is the nameless, faceless, indescribable No-Thing
that is the mysterious source and ground of all. Many of us call this
One *God* or, in Masonic terms, the *Great Architect of the Universe*.

In some way that defies our complete understanding, apart
from creation of the universe as we know it, within that Transcendent Monad there is the "will," or an "intention," for the freedom of
otherness to be. Some of humanity's creation myths try to explain why
this happens, yet others leave it as a mystery. The story of Genesis does
not overtly explain the Divine's motive for creation; we are only given

a mythic beginning of space-time in which the Great Architect first creates the distinction of heaven and earth. From this basic duality of heaven and earth arises all the amazing diversity in the tapestry of creation. Furthermore, all of it is declared good, which is to say that, at least so far, things are as they should be. There is an incalculable multitude of things, but their diversity does not obscure the fact of their common source, their intimate interconnectedness, their overarching and completely integrated, harmonious unity.

Despite the multiplicity of forms in creation, careful reading of scripture and firsthand knowledge of the mystical experiences they are based upon reveals that all is one. Everything and everyone lives, moves, and has their being in the same Ultimate Reality, the Absolute, or God. There is nowhere that the One is not. Yet, in our divinely endowed freedom to pursue the depths of otherness, we can suffer a kind of intoxication and thus fail to perceive our unity with the One and All. The self-other dichotomy becomes a veil on unity, a distraction from the wholeness of the Mystic Tie, and is thus distorted into the illusion of an absolute separateness.

The development of this illusion of separation is one way to understand the symbolism of Adam's lonely wish for a companion, temptation for knowledge of good and evil, eating the forbidden fruit, trying to hide from God, and the consequential ejection from Eden. In each of these developments, the distinction between heaven and earth is further magnified until it is an opposition of two disconnected worlds, one pure and one corrupt. Even so, behind the veil of this myth of humanity's fall is the truth that it is not actually a departure from God's presence and grace, but rather the loss of an *intimate awareness* of God, a descent into forgetfulness of our indissoluble unity with Ultimate Reality. That illusion of separation and its consequences are, at least among humans, infectious and self-propagating, and perhaps this provides the greatest significance to the popular concept of an "original sin" that is passed on from one generation to the next.

When we are completely aware of our communion with the Great Architect and all of creation, we have no needs; there is only That. Needs arise from the desire to either perpetuate the illusion of separateness or to overcome it and more fully know our unity with the One and All. Desire is thereby revealed as more fundamental than need in our existence. Even the need to survive disappears if one either no longer desires to live or recognizes that our existence transcends our physical and personal survival.

Our illusion of separation is at odds with our latent memory, or intuitive knowledge, of the Mystic Tie's unity; it is a dissonance, an incongruity, felt by us as incompleteness. It is the root of all uneasiness, all discomfort with self and others. In Genesis, this uncomfortable feeling of lack and need goes hand in hand with the illusion of separateness, as revealed in all the sufferings of Adam and Eve and their offspring.

Out of our deeply buried knowledge of unity as truth, desires emerge to eliminate the discomfort that accompanies the perception of lacking and needing. Yet, because such desires are felt and addressed within the illusory context of separation, they are distorted into desires to protect, defend, and even expand self as a separate entity, because self is perceived as the most immediate thing, and thus seems least illusory. Acting in response to the feeling of lack and the desires to protect, defend, and expand self, we then attempt to relieve the discomfort of this illusion through acquiring and possessing others (people, things, ideas, experiences, etc.), with the mistaken notion that we need them to fill the perceived emptiness. Thus, we can ironically perpetuate and compound the illusion of self's separateness, which in turn further fuels the desire for more acquisition and possession. Here is the core dynamic of all greed, gluttony, wantonness, and psychological addiction.

Others acting to acquire and possess in their own misguided self-interest interferes with our acquiring and possessing, even completely preventing or undoing our acquiring and possessing. Rather than collaborate with all for mutual benefit, we conclude that some others must be outperformed, if not eliminated, for self and those it identifies with to protect, defend, and expand themselves as fully as possible. Here is the fundamental mechanism of all envy, jealousy, cruelty, and war.

Every step reinforces and compounds the previous steps, and thus our energies spiral out into an ever larger, more complex, and more unmanageable chain of illusions and consequences. Yet, every step also offers the possibility of awakening to these illusions and more completely remembering the Mystic Tie, even if it is only because one's house of cards finally falls from its own weight and instability.

Some people insist that the basic phenomenon of otherness is either a cosmic mistake or a flaw in the spirit of humanity. The apparent fact of duality, the self-other binary that is at the very crux of creation, is judged as the fundamental evil that makes all of creation corrupt, and thus this world is regarded as a kind of prison to be endured. Hand in hand with that view may also be a sense of justification for indulging our vices or disregarding any care or concern for others, if not both. Alternately, this way of thinking may lead to the militant pursuit of an idealized world in which all distinctions of otherness, and thus all differences, particularly among human beings, are eliminated. It is, in effect, a misguided attempt to eliminate diversity and establish universal conformity to some imagined state of utopian homogeneity, which may be of either the political left or right, either religious or secular.

Unless we take the view that the God of Genesis is a deluded and megalomaniacal demiurge bent on making a cosmic mistake, which is nowhere recommended in regular Masonry, then we cannot conclude from Genesis that the basic duality of creation is an evil to be undone or fled. Instead, this creation myth suggests that the primary problem is our inebriation with our own otherness, and the authorities of many traditions promise that it is possible to overcome, or be delivered from, this problem. It might seem paradoxical, but they call us to return to awareness of unity while still participating in duality.

LUCIDITY

Lucid dreaming is an apt analogy for a state of being in which one has awareness of the Mystic Tie's unity while still participating in duality; in lucid dreaming, one knows one is dreaming while the dream is happening. It is a state less enmeshed in the illusions of separateness between self and the various others experienced in the dream, and yet the dream and one's presence in it may continue to manifest.

Anyone who experiences dream lucidity knows what a liberating moment it can be as the previously unquestioned dualities of a dream are more clearly known to be differing expressions of the mind doing the dreaming. What may have, only seconds before, seemed like an unbearable nightmare can suddenly be experienced with a light heart, even a sense of humor, not unlike a carnival house of horrors, or even be completely transformed into an experience of peace and serenity. More pleasant dreams can have their beauty magnified as the wonder and awe of their mysterious artistry is more deeply appreciated. Imagine what it is like to realize in lucidity that the mind is somehow mysteriously creating and sustaining an entire world around you, and with incredible vibrancy and detail. A monotonous repetition of typical events can be seized as an opportunity to break the laws of physics and joyously fly in the air or peacefully breathe underwater. Almost anything is possible, and no ugliness seems quite as genuinely threatening to you or any other in the dream.

Mystical insight, enlightenment, revelation, or whatever you want to call it, can impart a similar liberation with our presence in the so-called "waking world." From a mystical perspective, our waking world is like a shared dream in which all our seemingly separate minds are participating with a consensus about how things work. Individuals who become lucid in this world attain some measure of liberation from those "rules," and thus find greater freedom to enjoy their unity with others and to artistically shape the world for themselves and others.

AWAKEN, DREAMER

Awaken, dreamer, awaken,

the dawn of a new day draws near.

Awaken still within your dream

to the call that none but you can hear.

For though many souls may fancy

that they are dreamlessly aware,

the most lucid know the waking world

is but the dream that we most share.

Our flickering reality

is a fire composed of many fires,

each of us its co-creators

according to our own desires.

So, awaken, dreamer, awaken,

for the spirit in you revives.

Awaken, still within your dream,

and thus the new day's dawn arrives.

Just as one can fade in and out of lucidity within a dream, we can do so in the waking world. One moment we can remember the Mystic Tie and enjoy our freedom in greater measure, and the very next moment again fall into the drunken dream of illusory separation. Therefore, the mechanisms of lucidity are, to some extent, apparently not entirely within our personal control, at least for most of us. On the other hand, the desire to experience lucidity, and the intention to maintain it, do seem to make a significant difference. If the great sages and seers of history have spoken truthfully, then there is not only a cave of shadows, but there are also paths of lucidity, time-tested ways of joyfully experiencing and exploring what we Masons call the Mystic Tie.

As noted, Genesis does not say why the Creator creates, only that God does so and regards it as good. We can therefore surmise that creation and our otherness are not evils to be destroyed, mistakes to be corrected, or a prison to be escaped. The Genesis myth further suggests that we are created in God's image, to be the Creator's partners in creation, with the potential to tend the Great Mystery's garden while directly aware of the Absolute's presence in all things at all times. In other words, we have the innate capacity to be more aware participants in manifesting the Monad's infinite possibilities in the All, to be lucid co-builders of this great multidimensional temple. In addition, we learn that we are endowed with freedom, for without it we would be severely limited in our ability to intentionally transform things from one state into something new and different, yet that freedom also makes it possible for us to forget and ignore our Mystic Tie with the One and All. So, when we ask why we experience duality, perhaps what we are really seeking is some understanding of what we *should* be doing with our otherness and freedom, as if that answer lies external to our own deepest and truest desires. If we are indeed created to be free co-creators, then the more meaningful question is this: In your heart of hearts, undeceived by the illusion of separation, lucidly aware of the Mystic Tie, what would you *want* to do with your otherness and freedom?

CONCLUSION

We have seen that Masonry's symbol of the Mystic Tie has profound possibilities of meaning far beyond the feelings and commitments of sincere kinship. Most compelling are the suggestions that it represents the oneness of all things with their Creator, that we can become more aware of and illuminated by that unity, and that Masonry offers us a way to do so. There are many more questions and implications we could continue to explore, such as what this view of the Mystic Tie suggests about our perceptions of good and evil, morality and immorality, and what they mean in every aspect of our lives – personal, social, political, and environmental. So, in closing this chapter, you are welcome to reflect upon a poem that arose from contemplation of the Mystic Tie.

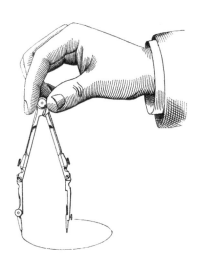

TRACING THE MYSTIC TIE

Tracing the Mystic Tie,

The mind moving the hand,

The hand holding the compass,

The compass tracing the circle,

The circle and the central point within,

The surface upon which they appear—

The meaning of each is only complete

In connection with every other.

Fully knowing any is knowing all.

Such knowing is love,

Loving the One

Loving the All.

All is Love.

Love is the One

Tracing the Mystic Tie.

CHAPTER TWO
MASONRY'S CONTEMPLATIVE PATH
TOWARD WHOLENESS

There is an important relationship between oneness and whole-ness. In fact, it is very hard to conceive of these qualities apart from each other. Even so, the concept of wholeness may be easier to grasp in the context of experiencing a multitude of things. Therefore, in this chapter we work with the idea of wholeness and the role contempla-tion plays in moving toward it. We presently explore this subject in a manner that is based on a contemplative method taught to the author many years ago. A teacher and mentor suggested that when we come upon a sentence or phrase that seems especially meaningful, thought provoking, or enigmatic, we should consider the words in reverse order, beginning with the last and proceeding to the first. Doing so can help us look deeper, not only into the significance of each word, but also into the relationships between the words.

WHOLENESS

The fifth word in the chapter's title is *wholeness*. An important thing to note about Masonry's view of wholeness is that it is not merely having all the parts of something gathered in one place, because all the parts can be piled together but the one thing itself not actually be fully and functionally present. So, for example, when the Temple of King Solomon was complete, all the parts are said to have "fit together with exact nicety." That fitting together turned a bunch of stones and timbers into one whole building consecrated for sacred purposes. That is how it became more than the sum of its parts, which is a hallmark of wholeness.

We know the Temple is a model for the lodge, and not only for the lodge room as a physical place, but for us as a group, the members coming together to make a whole social entity. Our ritual teaches that we should work to ensure all parts of that social entity fit together with exact nicety when it reminds us that the chief strength and support of all well-regulated organizations is peace and harmony, but this analogy of the Temple's wholeness does not stop with the lodge. We enter a deeper layer of symbolism when we consider that the Temple, and thus the lodge, is also a model for each of us as an individual human being.

Each of us is an assembly of parts, not only in the members and organs of our bodies, but throughout our being. We are physical, emotional, intellectual, and spiritual creatures, all at the same time.

Those are the four major elements of our individual being, and they have both conscious and unconscious aspects. While they may all be present together in one psyche, it takes only a little reflection to recall how they do not always fit together with exact nicety, how peace and harmony among them can wane, even seem to totally disappear, and sometimes for excruciatingly lengthy periods of time. We all know what that is like. We speak of being torn about something, of feeling conflicted, of being at odds with ourselves. Despite our best intentions otherwise, we can do or say things we wish we had not, or not do or not say things we wish we had. In such moments we are more fragmented, less integrated, less whole, but the extent to which the various parts of an individual are working together in peace and harmony is the extent to which one is more whole, more than the sum of one's own parts.

One thing inherent to this understanding of wholeness is that it is not an all or nothing condition. Rather, we can experience more or less wholeness from moment to moment. So, our Craft acknowledges that we have a natural desire for the peace and harmony of a more fully integrated and actualized wholeness in our lives, some measure of liberation from the illusions of separateness and lacking. Indeed, Masonry encourages us to pick up our tools and work toward fulfillment of that desire.

TOWARD

So, we have come to the fourth word of our title, *toward*. It is important for us to keep in mind that we can always be working toward a greater wholeness, making general progress in it, but with the understanding that the work is never finished so long as we live in this world. We need to remember we are fallible human beings with minds that are simply incapable of fully grasping all the complexity and mystery of our own existence. Our lucidity waxes and wanes, and we are going to make mistakes. We will inevitably grow tired, have moments of weakness, succumb to the effects of aging, and often simply fail to see and understand all the relevant factors and consequences for many of our decisions and actions.

Keeping these realities in mind is important because it helps to spare us from two follies that often befall people seeking to better themselves. One of those follies is the unnecessary and unhealthy self-loathing and self-punishment that typically goes hand in hand with unrealistic expectations of ourselves. The other folly is the grandiose delusion of having arrived at some degree of completion or perfection from which we can never fall. It is also very much worth noting that the less we plague ourselves with these follies, and the more accepting and understanding we are of our own humanity, the more prepared we are to be accepting of and compassionate with the humanity of others. Like the Temple of Solomon, the vision of existing in the wholeness of peace, harmony, and unity, lucidly experiencing and joyfully expressing the Mystic Tie, is meant to inspire us to do the best we can with what we have, to persevere in the work, and to renew our efforts when we fail. This includes learning from our experiences and making changes that reflect our hard-won wisdom.

Path

Arriving at our title's third word, recall Claudy's assertion that Masonry is a *way* to God. Masonry provides us with a *path* to follow in this quest toward wholeness, a way of oneness traveled by others who have gone before us. Furthermore, our tradition gives us many instructions about how to travel that path, complete with milestones and elder brethren to help us know where we are and how to better manage whatever we encounter.

For now, let us construct a basic outline for how to travel that path as a three-step process that would be familiar to the craftsman of any trade. First, we must be *aware* of our tools, materials, and designs, or the parts that make up the whole of our being. Second, we must try to *understand* how the parts relate to each other, developing our comprehension of their proper relationships with each other within the whole that is greater than the sum of its parts. Third, we must combine our understandings with deliberate actions to initiate *manifestation* of the designs into reality. We may then experiment with the parts, adjusting them and their connections to more harmoniously integrate them, refining them further and further toward a state of exact nicety. By outlining this three-step path of awareness, understanding, and manifestation we come to *contemplative*, the second word in our title.

CONTEMPLATIVE

Following Masonry's way of oneness and path toward wholeness *is* a contemplative process, which is to say that it is one in which we are intentionally directing our consciousness toward deeper awareness, understanding, and manifestation of the truths communicated by our tradition. The rituals themselves are meant to draw and hold our reverent attention on profound symbols and concepts, and they urge us to unfold and develop their meanings in our lives. We can amplify the process through contemplative practices like the art of memory, mindfulness, meditation, prayer, study, and dialogue.[4]

Because our Craft is religiously pluralistic and inclusive, we should consider the fact that contemplative practice is extoled by many of the great spiritual books and teachers in history:

> *I commune with my heart in the night; I meditate and search my spirit. (David, King of Israel)*

---

4. See the appendix for instructions on developing mystical interpretations of Masonic symbols. For a more thorough exploration of contemplative methods applied in Craft Lodge Masonry, see Dunning, Jr., C.R., (2016). *Contemplative Masonry: Basic Applications of Mindfulness, Meditation, and Imagery for the Craft*. Stone Guild.

From meditation wisdom arises, and without meditation wisdom wanes. (The Buddha)

Contemplation for one hour is better than formal worship for sixty years. (The Prophet Muhammad)

In the still mind, in the depths of meditation, the Eternal Self reveals itself. (Krishna)

Attain utmost vacuity; hold fast to quietude. This reversion belongs to the eternal. To know the eternal is enlightenment. (Lao Tse)

Through the faculty of meditation man attains to eternal life; through it he receives the breath of the Holy Spirit—the bestowal of the Spirit is given in reflection and meditation. ('Abdu'l-Bahá)

The Kingdom of Heaven is within you. Seek first the Kingdom of Heaven. (Jesus of Nazareth)

MASONRY

So, now let us reflect on how our Craft uniquely encourages us to make such contemplative effort on its path toward wholeness and lucidity in the Mystic Tie. In fact, our tradition not only encourages but strongly admonishes us to do so. Consider the following statements from the monitor of the Grand Lodge of Texas.

Initiation is to be attained only after real labor, deep study, profound meditation, extensive research and a constant practice of those virtues which will open a true path to moral, intellectual, and spiritual illumination.

Masonry does not expound the truths concealed in her emblems. It displays the symbols and may give a hint here and there concerning some characteristic of its several meanings, but it must remain for the Neophite to search out for himself the more hidden significations.

It [the Lodge] is said to be opened on, and not in, a certain degree, in reference rather to the speculative, than to the legal character, of the meeting; to indicate, not that the members are to be circumscribed in the limits of a particular degree, but that they are met together to unite in contemplation on the symbolic teachings and divine lessons, to inculcate which is the peculiar object of that degree.

He who would become an accomplished Mason must not be content merely to hear or even to understand the lectures, but must, aided by them and then having as it were the way marked out for him, study, interpret, and develop these symbols for himself.

Widely recorded in most Masonic monitors is this teaching on one of our principal tenets:

Truth is a divine attribute, and the foundation of every virtue. To be good and true is the first lesson we are taught in Masonry. On this theme we contemplate, and by its dictates endeavor to regulate our conduct.

When explaining the special nature of Speculative Masonry, our monitors say:

It leads the contemplative to view with reverence and admiration the glorious works of creation, and inspires him with the most exalted ideas of the perfection of his divine Creator. Our ancient brethren, in obedience to God's law, labored six days and rested on the seventh, thereby enjoying frequent opportunities to contemplate the glorious works of the creation, and to adore the Great Creator.

In fact, the traditional opening charge of many lodges is this:

The ways of Virtue are beautiful. Knowledge is attained by degrees. Wisdom dwells with contemplation. There we must seek her.

In his *Encyclopedia of Freemasonry*, the Masonic scholar Albert Mackey further clarifies the relevance of contemplation to Masonry when he writes:

*To contemplate is, literally, to watch and inspect the Temple. The augur, or prophet, among the Romans, having taken his stand on the Capitoline Hill, marked out with his wand the space in the heavens he intended to consult. This space he called the **templum**, the Latin word for a designated or marked-off area. [...] The watching of the templum was called **contemplating**; and hence those who devoted themselves to meditation upon sacred subjects assumed this title. [...] Among the Freemasons, the word **speculative** is used as equivalent to **contemplative**.*

Mackey was right about these words *speculative* and *contemplative*. The root of the word *speculate* is the same root for *spectacles*, the eyeglasses we use to see more clearly. Thus, at the time when our forebearers began describing themselves as speculative Masons, the word *speculative* literally meant "looking into" the vast and deep possibilities of meaning in Masonic symbolism, which is an effort to see the truth of things more lucidly. Therefore, *speculative* was indeed equivalent in meaning to be *contemplative*, and it should remain so for today's Mason.

It is important to understand that contemplation is not only deeper and more focused thinking about something, but also includes meditatively opening our hearts and minds to wisdom through intuition and inspiration. This is an especially important issue for mystics and Masons. Intuition is far more than a knee-jerk reaction or a conclusion based on superficial observations. That common misunderstanding of intuition is based on the notion that empirical reasoning is the highest function of the human intellect. So, the popular meaning of the word *intuition* has become conflated with that of *assumption*, which is why people now often say something is "counterintuitive" to signify that it is different than they expected or assumed it would be. However, in the classical sense and the mystical sense, intuition is the experience of information entering awareness from outside of our ordinary mental process. It is most noticeable when we have acknowledged that we cannot find what we want or need in our memories, through following chains of association, or by reasoning, and so we have opened our minds to a receptive state in which we can experience the arrival of something that begins to unfold in our awareness. When this is done prayerfully, we are engaging the process described by Jesus in Matthew 6:6 (ASV):

> *But thou, when thou prayest, enter into thine inner chamber, and having shut thy door, pray to thy Father who is in secret, and thy Father who seeth in secret shall recompense thee.*

The inner chamber referenced in this passage is mystically understood to be one's own mind, and the act of shutting the door is the process of turning our attention inward, away from our sensations, perceptions, thoughts, and feelings about external things. The "secret" here is the sacred silence that is so often hidden deep within us. As a parallel, recall how our legend says that Hiram Abiff would retire to pray in the unfinished Sanctum Sanctorum before drawing his designs on the trestleboard. Contemplation of this sort is a profoundly spiritual pursuit, and any intuition received is a gift of more light.[5]

So far, we have been focusing on the personal inner work of Masonry's contemplative path toward wholeness. That is an appropriate starting place, because in our tradition it is the internal and not the external that recommends one to be made a Mason. Yet, once we enter the lodge, we are constantly urged not only to work on ourselves for our own benefit, but also to work for the improvement of our relationships and society. In countless ways, our Craft teaches us that wholeness is something we should not only work toward internally, but also externally, because we are social beings. For example, let us recall this lesson on hearing from the Fellow Craft Degree, noticing the various parts and dimensions of our being, internal and external, that it addresses.

> *Hearing is that sense by which we distinguish sounds and are capable of appreciating the agreeable charms of music. By it, we are enabled to enjoy the pleasures of society, and reciprocally to communicate to each other our thoughts and intentions, our purposes and desires; and thus our reason is rendered capable of exerting its utmost power and energy. The wise and beneficent Author of Nature intended, by the formation of this sense, that we should be social creatures, and receive the greatest and most important part of our knowledge from social intercourse with each other. For these purposes we are endowed with hearing, that, by a proper exertion of our rational powers, our happiness may be complete.*

Let us also revisit a portion of the Master Mason's lecture on the beehive, which says:

---

5. For more on intuition in mysticism, see Griffon, C. (n.d.). "Intuition: An Essential Element of Mysticism," *Confraternity of the Rose Cross.* https://www.crcsite.org/rosicrucian-library/expanded-collection/intuition/

It might have pleased the great Creator of heaven and earth to have made man independent of all other beings; but, as dependence is one of the strongest bonds of society, mankind were made dependent upon each other for protection and security, as they thereby enjoy better opportunities of fulfilling the duties of reciprocal love and friendship. Thus was man formed for social and active life; the noblest part of the work of God....

These are just two of the ways Masonry reminds us that the internal elements of our individual being and the external aspects of our social being are interwoven and inseparable parts of an even greater wholeness we are working to realize.

So, when we follow Masonry's contemplative path toward wholeness by trying to improve ourselves and realize our unity with others, by practicing awareness, understanding, and thoughtful manifestation of wholeness within ourselves and in our relationships with others, what do we call that? Is there a single word aside from *Masonry* that sums it all up? The teaching on the beehive points to this question's answer by encouraging us to "enjoy better opportunities of fulfilling the duties of reciprocal love and friendship." In short, the one word that best describes Masonry's contemplative path toward wholeness is *love*.

Love is the great work that our Craft repeatedly urges us to contemplatively engage both internally and externally. The importance of love in Masonry is punctuated by the fact that the very last tool presented to a Master Mason is the Trowel, which spreads the cement of Brotherly Love and affection. But by this juncture in the Masonic quest, the new Master Mason has already been taught many other lessons about love. Let us review some of the more obvious ones.

Soon after entering the lodge for initiation, the Entered Apprentice (EA) hears these words: "Behold how good and how pleasant it is for brethren to dwell together in unity." And what do those words describe if not a relationship among members so loving that they regard each other as family? The EA is taught about the three Principal Tenets of Truth, Relief, and Brotherly Love. And while the latter tenet directly addresses love, both Relief and Truth are described in terms that emphasize their roles in loving relationships. The EA is dramatically reminded about the importance of Charity as it is expressed through Relief. In learning about the covering of the lodge, the initiate is taught that the highest of the Three Theological Virtues is Charity, and that the infinite reaches of the lodge's symbolic form suggest the extent to which one's own Charity should reach.

With all this emphasis on Charity in our Craft, we should take a moment to examine it more carefully. The English word *Charity* comes from the Latin *caritas*, which was used in translation of the original Greek *agape* in the Apostle Paul's 1st letter to the Corinthians. We get our Three Theological Virtues from the thirteenth chapter of 1st Corinthians, which is an exposition on the nature of love and its supreme importance. It is the chapter that begins:

> *Though I speak with the tongues of men and of angels, but have not love, I have become only sounding brass or a clanging cymbal. And though I have the gift of prophecy, and understand all mysteries and all knowledge, and though I have all faith, so that I could remove mountains, but have not love, I am nothing. And though I bestow all my goods to feed the poor, and though I give my body to be burned so I may boast, but have not love, it profits me nothing.*

At the end of that chapter, Paul says that after everything else fails, three things remain – faith, hope, and love – and then he clarifies that love is the greatest of the three. The Greek word he used for love was *agape*, meaning selfless universal love, not just generosity. It was later translated into Latin as *caritas*, which was then translated in some English versions of the Bible as *charity*, while others rendered it as *love*. In any case, the Theological Virtue of Charity is about more than generosity; it is about love in its wholeness.

Getting back to how our Craft teaches about love, the previous examples were some of the more obvious. Since we began with the last tool of the Master Mason, let us go a little deeper by contemplating the first tools of the Entered Apprentice. Consider the 24-inch Gauge, which teaches us to divide our time into a portion for our usual occupations, a portion for service to God and distressed brethren, and a portion for rest and refreshment. Here we can see three divisions of loving effort. The portion for work is done to seek wages that we may better provide and care for others and ourselves, which is a loving thing. It may also be that we see our occupations themselves as forms of loving service to others. The portion for service to God and distressed brethren is a demonstration of our love for both, and the portion for rest and refreshment is an act of love for ourselves, as well as others, by ensuring we have the health and energy needed for the other two portions. Regarding the lesson of the Common Gavel, it is very much a labor of love for ourselves and for others when we strive to divest ourselves of our vices and superfluities. While they are not tools in the physical sense, we should also consider things like the Four Cardinal Virtues and the Liberal Arts and Sciences. Each of them empowers us to be more loving of ourselves, other people, or the Divine in some way, and the work of empowering ourselves with them is itself an act of love.

All the way through every degree of Masonry in every rite, every symbolic working tool and every resource is an instrument of love. In other words, *everything about Masonry is meant to support our awareness, understanding, and manifestation of wholeness with love.* Each symbol offers a means to be more loving in our actions, in how we manage our emotions, in the way we think, and in the way we relate to others and the Great Architect of the Universe. It is very appropriate that Masonry teaches us these things in the symbolism and allegory of a craft, because a craft requires work.

Taken as a whole, the great diversity of tools and resources on the Masonic path illustrates that love is much more than feelings like attraction and affection, and it demands much more from us than emotions, requiring virtues like prudence, temperance, fortitude, justice, faith, and hope. Just like our souls, love is multidimensional; it can be experienced and expressed physically, emotionally, intellectually, and spiritually. One way this multidimensionality is demonstrated is by the fact that we can think loving thoughts or do loving things even when we do not *feel* loving in the moment. However, because the wholeness of love itself includes all the different ways we can experience and express it, the more we give ourselves to awareness, understanding, and manifesting love through contemplative practices like study, meditation, the art of memory, prayer, and dialogue, then the more love facilitates our own wholeness, transforming us both internally and externally. Indeed, such contemplative practice is love in action.

When we talk about love, it is quite easy to take the attitude that it is just a touchy-feely thing, flowing naturally in warmth, sweetness, and coziness, or not at all, but that is a one-sided view of love. The fact is that it can be hard work, true labor, to discipline ourselves so that we manage our emotions lovingly, think loving thoughts, make loving decisions, take loving action, and respond with loving attitudes regardless of things going as we would prefer or not. A commitment to live this way is hardly always easy or pleasant, and we all know that.

Masonry's contemplative path toward wholeness, our loving Craft, can be arduous, and so it is meant for grown up adults who are willing to give themselves to the heroic quest of transformation into strong, wise, and beautifully loving elders. The Builder's Art is not designed to be a mere pastime for people unwilling to be divergent and critical thinkers, and to outgrow lesser notions about who and what they are. Mature adults know that love presents us with challenges and conflicts, such as when we deeply care about people or things that clash with each other. Within the context of our illusory separation from the Divine and others in creation, love brings us struggle, frustration, disappointment, grief, and regret in addition to all the beautiful, sweet, and thrilling things of life, and we ought to remember that truth every time we see or speak of our Checkered Pavement.

In becoming more lucid in love, coming to terms with its diverse and complex nature, learning that love is always present, realizing that it flows through both the pleasant and unpleasant moments of life, we can discover one of the great mysteries about love, which is its transcendence. Love has no opposite that can overcome it. Though we often speak of fear or hate as the opposite of love, we should note that these are the names of feelings and, as we have seen, love is much more than a feeling. We can feel fear or hate and still think and do loving things despite those feelings. We can always find a way to directly engage with love itself because, in its fullness, love is both ever-present and transcendent, which is to say it is Divine. Love is thus a very powerful way to wholeness, harmony, and unity, as has been extoled by the sages of many traditions.

Dear friends, let us love one another, for love comes from God. Everyone who loves has been born of God and knows God. Whoever does not love does not know God, because God is love. [...] No one has ever seen God; but if we love one another, God lives in us and his love is made complete in us. (St. John the Evangelist)

When your mind is filled with love, send it in one direction, then a second, a third, and a fourth, then above, and then below. Identify with everything, without hatred, resentment, anger, or enmity. This mind of love is wide. It grows immeasurably and eventually is able to embrace the whole world. (The Buddha)

Love is the thing that binds and attaches man to his Creator, increasing his spiritual strength, and enveloping him with an aura of the Divine. The main element of such love is the joy in one's heart, the flaming of the soul before its Creator, and the devotion of all one's powers to sanctify God's Name and fulfill His Will. (Moshe Chaim Luzatto)

God is love, and love is the panacea for human suffering. There is nothing greater than love – God's quality of attraction and unity that is manifested in the soul of every being. (Paramahansa Yogananda)

Be drunk on love, because love is all that exists; without love, no one has the right to enter His house. [...] It is Love and the Lover that live eternally – do not lend your heart to anything else; all else is borrowed. How long will you go on and on embracing a corpse? Embrace the soul that is embraced by nothing else. (Mathnawi)

You should know that Love himself is the cause of his being discovered: that Love which we have now found here. For once our desire to find Love had been kindled by Love, we sought Love and found Love. This is why our thanks for seeking and finding him must go to Love himself for his incomparable loving kindness. Oh, how wonderful is the splendor of this God of Love! [...] Love offers himself to us even before we start looking for him. [...] Therefore, my friends, let us worship this divine Love which is so kind and favorable to us; let us worship it in such a way that we come to revere the Wisdom of God and stand in awe and wonder before the Power of God, and thus, through Love, receive the favor of the Godhead in its entirety; and, by loving the Godhead in its entirety by means of Love, we may enjoy it all with everlasting Love. (Marsilio Ficino)

Know thou of a certainty that Love is the secret of God's holy Dispensation, the manifestation of the All-Merciful, the fountain of spiritual outpourings. Love is heaven's kindly light, the Holy Spirit's eternal breath that vivifieth the human soul.

Love is the cause of God's revelation unto man, the vital bond inherent, in accordance with the divine creation, in the realities of things. Love is the one means that ensureth true felicity both in this world and the next. Love is the light that guideth in darkness, the living link that uniteth God with man, that assureth the progress of every illumined soul. Love is the most great law that ruleth this mighty and heavenly cycle, the unique power that bindeth together the divers elements of this material world, the supreme magnetic force that directeth the movements of the spheres in the celestial realms. Love revealeth with unfailing and limitless power the mysteries latent in the universe. Love is the spirit of life unto the adorned body of mankind, the establisher of true civilization in this mortal world, and the shedder of imperishable glory upon every high-aiming race and nation. ('Abdu'l-Bahá)

Love is always holding out its hand to lead us out of the illusory depths of separation and lack and into more lucid oneness in the Mystic Tie. Love is therefore not only Masonry's path toward internal and external wholeness – it is the very essence of the peace and harmony that our Craft holds up as the ideal for human existence at all levels. In other words, love is at once the destination of our path, the traveling of our path, and the path itself. Love is our work, Love is our wage, and Love is our Mystic Tie.

Given this realization, the ever-present questions for us are about how committed we are to work at Masonry's craft of love and fully engage its contemplative way of oneness and path toward greater wholeness and lucidity in the Mystic Tie. So, how willing are we to keep looking for and opening to deeper awareness of ourselves and our relationships with others and with the Divine? How willing are we to keep striving for a better understanding of wholeness? How willing are we to keep manifesting the most loving things?

THIS HOLY FLAME

Upon this old, checkered pavement we stand,

Brothers united in the Master's plan.

Reflecting, we circle this sacred ground,

Seeking our wholeness in silence profound.

Committed we are to aspire, ascend,

To tend to our souls, to heal and to mend.

With thoughts, and feelings, and spirit aligned,

And actions conformed to timeless designs,

We open our minds to deep inner sight,

Each exploring our bonds with Love's pure light.

Listening to Wisdom, we ponder the quest,

To desire and choose what is truly best.

With hearts wide open, we strive to conceive

The banner of life that Beauty would weave.

Grateful and humble, we kneel, and we pray,

Then with Strength unyielding we tread the way,

And through veils of time we'll ever persist,

To commune in Love's glow, to coexist.

So, brothers, let us keep this Holy Flame,

In the Mystic Tie, by the Hallowed Name –

With compassion our compass and our creed,

We'll assemble the Temple with Love's lead,

Until all souls under the moon and sun

Welcome each other and know we're all one.

Chapter Three
Gnothi Seauton – *You are the Mysteries!*

In its most superficial sense, the term *mysteries* simply refers to things about Masonry that are concealed or hidden, at least hypothetically, from those who are uninitiated. Because so many details of our initiatic rites are meant to be kept secret in this way, the word *mysteries* has at times been used as a synonym for the rites themselves. In that regard, Masonry is like the Mystery Schools of the ancient world. For thousands of years, cultures like the Romans, Greeks, and Egyptians maintained rites of religious and philosophical education that were provided only to initiates, or *mystae* in Greek, who were sworn to secrecy. There is a deeper sense in which the word *mysteries* is fitting for those ancient traditions, and to dig into that sense we can consult the works of Plato, student of Socrates and teacher of Aristotle.

Plato was undoubtedly an initiate, and scholars have strongly suspected that his work contains ideas and inspirations from his experience of the Mysteries. For instance, in the dialogue *Phaedo*, Plato has Socrates praising initiated philosophers when he says, "to be numbered amongst whom I have bent all the effort of a lifetime." According to Plato, the highest intention of the Mysteries was to facilitate initiates' contemplative discovery of the Intelligible Realm, for it is only there that we find the true nature of things and their source. Plato makes it clear that the Intelligible Realm is metaphysical or spiritual, transcending our ordinary sense perceptions and habitual ways of thinking, and so it usually seems hidden or concealed from us. Thus, the Ancient Mysteries were not only mysterious because their inner workings were kept secret, but also because their rites and teachings addressed humanity's timeless questions about the mysterious truths of things like life, death, rebirth, the nature of the soul, and even the essential truth of existence itself. If, as Plato insists, the greatest knowledge of such things lies beyond our ordinary ways of thinking, then the manner of teaching about them must also be extraordinary. This is why the Ancient Mysteries taught through ritual, myth, and symbol, just as Masonry does.

So far, we have already seen parallels between the Ancient Mysteries and Masonry. We have specifically noted that both traditions have required initiation and oaths of secrecy, and both have used ritual, myth, and symbol as means of teaching. The most significant question now is whether they share a common purpose. Do the rites and teachings of Masonry intentionally provide their initiates with opportunities to contemplate the ideals of mysterious things like life, death, rebirth, the nature of the soul, and even the essential truth of existence itself?

Many Masonic scholars and authors have answered that question with a resounding *yes*. Some of them have gone into detail on the subject, and the most conscientious of them have agreed with Joseph Fort Newton when he writes:

> *Masonry stands in this tradition; and if we may not say that it is historically related to the great ancient orders, it is their* **spiritual** *descendant, and renders much the same ministry to our age which the Mysteries rendered to the olden world. [...] This at least is true: the Greater Ancient Mysteries were prophetic of Masonry whose drama is an epitome of universal initiation, and whose simple symbols are the depositaries of the noblest wisdom of mankind. As such, it brings men together at the altar of prayer, keeps alive the truths that make us men, seeking, by every resource of art, to make tangible the power of love, the worth of beauty, and the reality of the ideal.*

So, having established the parallel, let us attempt to pass through the door of the Ancient Mysteries, get to the most central concern of their myths and symbolism, and see how that relates with the mysteries of our Craft and to oneness, wholeness, harmony, and love. Of course, the mixed blessing of myths and symbols is that they conceal as well as reveal their deeper meanings. Myths and symbols are subject to speculation and interpretation, which can be limited to ordinary ways of thinking despite the intentions of the teachers who devised them. In another of Plato's dialogues, *Phaedrus*, Socrates talks about problems arising from interpretations that attempt to take the Mysteries' myths and symbols as speaking only of historical events and physical realities. He says: "I have no leisure for such enquiries; shall I tell you why? I must first know myself, as the Delphian inscription says...." Thus, we have come to the first part of this chapter's title, *Gnothi Seauton*, meaning "know thyself." This admonition was inscribed in the forecourt of the Temple of Delphi in ancient Greece, a place where an entranced priestess would speak a prophecy in response to a seeker's question. Imagine that! You have gone in search of divinely inspired guidance, and before you even enter the temple you are reminded to know yourself.

Socrates references this inscription in saying the Mysteries inspire him to work at knowing himself rather than to try making literal sense of their myths and symbols. A more extensive aphorism of this nature has been attributed to our friend and brother, Pythagoras, who influenced Plato: "Man know thyself; then thou shalt know the Universe and God." This statement is significant because it clarifies that self-knowledge is not only of the utmost importance, but more specifically that it is the key to knowing the transcendent truths that were the highest aim of the Ancient Mysteries. Note that it implies the wholeness of a human being reflects the wholeness of creation, and that there is a oneness of our nature with that of the Creator.

This key to the most profound wisdom has its parallels in other ancient traditions. For example, in Kabbalah we are reminded that the book of Genesis says we are created in the image of God and with the breath of God. It is further explained that the essential light of each soul is a spark of the Divine Light. It is thus a Kabbalistic principle that the more we contemplate the nature and dynamics of the soul, the better we understand the nature and dynamics of creation, and thus the better we know our Creator. This Kabbalistic principle is mirrored in the Hermetic Axiom, *as above, so below*, which is quoted in some of our rites. Likewise, in Vedanta, the ancient wisdom tradition of India, we find the saying, *Tat Tvam Asi*, translated as "Thou art That," meaning the true self in you, your spiritual essence, is one with the Divine Self.

In other words, the mysteries of the self are inextricably intertwined with the mysteries of existence and the mysteries of the Divine. So, you *are* the mysteries! Remember that we came to this light in consideration of whether the central focus of the Masonic mysteries is the same as that of the Ancient Mysteries. Thus, the question has become whether our Craft urges us to contemplate the most essential and mysterious things about ourselves.

To begin answering that question, let us revisit the kinds of questions repeatedly asked from the onset of initiation and throughout the experience of our degrees. Without using the specific language of our ritual, Masons should recognize their similarities to these questions, which all thoughtful people ask themselves from time to time:

Who are you?

Where do you come from?

Why are you here?

Where are you going?

What are you looking for?

Why is that important to you?

While our ritual prescribes answers that harken back to the past of operative masonry, we should recall that we are Speculative Masons and thus recognize the traditional answers are meant to be mythic and symbolic. If we take the questions seriously, regarding them and their answers as more than a ritual formality, then we can easily see how each question directs us straight back to ourselves, for it is only within ourselves that we can find our most genuine, authentic, and unprescribed answers. So, instead of responding to "Who are you?" with the ritually prescribed answer, I might answer by saying that my name is Chuck, that I am the son of Buddy and Joyce, I am married to Susan, I am an American, and a Mason. I could go on to list my vocation, religion, ethnicity, and so on. Answers like these are important, but they still have not crossed the threshold of ordinary thinking that Plato says we must cross to approach the most real. Leaving behind all the ordinary answers we might have, and thus descending into the deeper depths of such questions, or ascending into their higher heights, we discover that they do indeed lead us beyond any easy answers and into the mysteries of our very existence.

Let us also consider that when a new Masonic initiate receives the first set of working tools, we clarify that a Mason is not only a worker, but also the material upon which the work is done. As is revealed in many of our monitors, we further explain the aim of the work is to make oneself more fitting for "that spiritual building—that house not made with hands—eternal in the heavens," which in Platonic terms is to realize our oneness with a metaphorical, metaphysical, archetypal temple in the Intelligible Realm. In that same presentation of these tools, we also teach that they represent principles by which one may self-regulate thoughts, attitudes, and conduct. These principles can only be understood and applied by our faculties of heart and mind, and so we can deduce that the most essential working tool of Masonry is *consciousness itself*. Consciousness is the tool that not only comprehends and applies all our other symbolic tools, but also produces them from itself. This concern is thus at the very core of the mysteries.

In accord with Socrates, Pythagoras, and thus the inscription at the Temple of Delphi, we have discovered that consciousness is the key to unlocking all the mysteries we can unlock, and it is therefore the point within the circle of all our work as Masons, just as it was in the Ancient Mysteries. It is the most essential mystery we seek to contemplatively reveal, or, in the symbolic language of our tradition, consciousness is Light and the Lost Word.

Now our primary question becomes this: How can we more intentionally and effectively engage this quest beyond the veils of or-dinary thinking and into the mysteries of consciousness? As a guide, Plato provides us with a divided line as an analogy for the wholeness of our consciousness as well as the way of oneness.

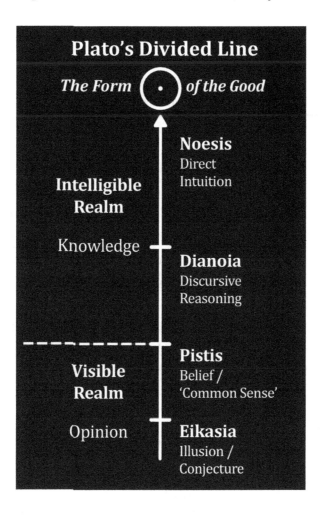

At the top of this line, you see the point within the circle and the words, *The Form of the Good.* In Plato's dialogues, forms are regarded as metaphysical or spiritual realities, the archetypes that give rise to, or are reflected by, things in social, psychological, and material existence. They are posited to be unchanging and eternal, and thus more real than things manifested in space and time, which are changing and temporary. Kabbalists have a similar theory about the nature of creation, which was influenced by Neoplatonic philosophy. In Kabbalah, creation continually emanates from the Godhead down through planes or worlds of manifestation. The highest of those worlds is called *Atzilut*, which literally means "emanation." At this level, there is only the radiation of Divine Light which has within it every design, or *form* in Plato's terminology, for all that can possibly exist. For this reason, contemporary Kabbalists sometimes speak of Atzilut as the "Archetypal World."

Plato suggests there is an Ultimate Form, a Supreme Archetype, that is the essential Divine Truth of all things. He calls that essential truth the *Form of the Good*, or simply *the Good*, because it is the cornerstone of all things, that which all things have in common and by which they are united. We hear a similar idea in the Apostle Paul's words to the Athenians in the New Testament Book of Acts, when he says God is that in which we live and move and have our being. In Plato's *Republic*, the Form of the Good is likened to the sun, radiating the light that makes life and sight possible in our physical world.

On the diagram, we have the point within the circle – the astronomical sign of the sun, the alchemical emblem of gold, the Pythagorean symbol of the Monad, and a fitting reminder of the Mystic Tie – representing the highest aim of initiated philosophers. The rest of the line represents a continuum of distinct kinds of thinking, faculties, or states of consciousness, illustrating the ascent of the way of oneness. It is divided into two general parts, the upper for the metaphysical Intelligible Realm, the realm of truest knowledge, and the lower for the Visible Realm where we experience things through the five senses, and where our understandings of them are opinions based on our limited perspectives.

In the Visible Realm, the bottom and shortest segment is labeled *Eikasia*, which literally means "imagination" in modern Greek. Plato was not referring to the mental faculty of imagination itself, but to the inability to distinguish between imagination and reality. The English words *illusion* and *conjecture* are placed here to offer clarity – *illusion* meaning that which is mistaken for being real, and *conjecture* meaning poorly informed guesswork taken as a basis for one's opinions and actions. This segment is where we are at our most ignorant and brutish, basically operating on autopilot, having knee-jerk reactions to almost everything. In terms of modern depth psychology, this is our state of mind when we are projecting our own unconscious assumptions, conflicts, biases, and repressed impulses onto the world around us rather than realizing and managing their presence within us. In this state, our consciousness of ourselves is almost completely limited to superficial awareness of our physical bodies and feelings of physical and emotional comfort or discomfort with things. These feelings form the basis of our opinions and attitudes, and we act out of them with little to no deliberation or reflection.

The next and somewhat longer segment in the Visible Realm is labeled *Pistis*, the Greek word for faith, trust, or belief. We have '*common sense*' printed on the diagram to clarify that at this level our opinions and attitudes are extensively shaped by what our cultures commonly implant into us and expect from us. This level is all about rules, political platforms, religious doctrines, and many other lists of dos and don'ts. So, here our thinking is a somewhat more sophisticated process of determining what opinions and attitudes, including about morality and ethics, are most congruent with our usual associates. We exercise self-awareness to the extent necessary to check our opinions, attitudes, and behaviors to get more of what we want and less of what we do not want in our particular social environment. Our faith, trust, and belief in what we have been conditioned to think and do can then become so habitual that we go back to operating on autopilot and having knee jerk reactions, but typically in conformity with and loyalty to our community's norms and a feeling of certainty about their correctness. However, not all societies are culturally homogenous, and thus in some there is less commonality. It is both a challenge and a benefit of cultural diversity that it makes it harder to sleepwalk through life with nothing but "common sense." Living with and embracing the diversity of humanity's wholeness, combined with an appreciation of the centrality of consciousness, constantly urges us to question ourselves and the powerful cultural influences on our views and feelings about things.

On that note, let us recall this beautiful statement about diversity in Masonry from Anderson's Constitutions:

> *...though in ancient Times Masons were charg'd in every Country to be of the Religion of that Country or Nation, whatever it was, yet 'tis now thought more expedient only to oblige them to that Religion in which all Men agree, leaving their particular Opinions to themselves; that is, to be good Men and true, or Men of Honour and Honesty, by whatever Denominations or Persuasions they may be distinguish'd; whereby Masonry becomes the Center of Union, and the Means of conciliating true Friendship among Persons that must have remain'd at a perpetual Distance.*

From a Platonic perspective, Anderson's exhortation to set aside "opinions," aim for a "center of Union," and facilitate "true" friendship, all suggest that he is calling for us to follow the way of oneness, crossing the threshold from the Visible Realm and common sense to move into the Intelligible Realm toward the Form of the Good. In doing so, we can contemplate and more clearly grasp the deeper realities and ideals upon which morality is based. We may even develop a higher knowledge and enjoyment of our unity in the transcendent Form of the Good, the ultimate essence of all things. In that light, the fraternal experience of the Mystic Tie that we speak of so fondly would be much more than sentiments of belonging, but rather a realization of the Good, the ideal form or archetype of unity, wholeness, and harmony, expressed in Brotherly Love.

We must first approach the threshold of the Intelligible Realm by beginning to question what we think we know, and then developing hypotheses about how things might be different than we have been told or previously understood. In short, our contemplations at this level are about speculating on different possibilities of meaning, and it is in the testing of those hypotheses that we can cross the threshold. Plato says the testing of our speculations is performed through *dianoia*, which we translate as "discursive reasoning." This kind of reasoning draws conclusions from information gained through the senses and mental images. In this context it includes critical thinking, making use of logic to better discern what can and cannot be true about something. When we apply this process to ourselves, we begin to ascertain the different faculties and dynamics of our own psyches, and the geometry of their relationships with each other.

One of the many things we can discover in such self-examination is that we are more mysterious to ourselves than we may have ever before noticed. We have dreams that perplex us. We feel emotions that surprise us. We do things despite our desires and intentions not to do them, and we do not do the things we desire and intend to do. We find that nearly everything we like to think of as permanent and unchanging about ourselves is, in fact, temporary and changing. Thus, from a Platonic perspective, we simply are not as real as we want to believe we are. Said another way, our self-concept, our notion of who and what we are, is not as truthful as it could be.

Even so, we can know without doubt that there is something absolutely true and permanent about our being. For example, following a contemplative process of observation and discursive thinking, the philosopher René Descartes arrived at his famous dictum, "I think therefore I am." This realization gets us a bit closer to the essential truth of our being. Descartes is not saying his thought makes him exist, but rather it is undeniable evidence of his mind, which is undeniable evidence of his existence. Yet thought, as we typically experience it, comes and goes and is ever changing, which is also true of our sense perceptions and emotions. With only Descartes's dictum to go on, then it might seem that in dreamless sleep we would cease to exist. So, we can come to understand that the most essential truth we perceive in the fact of our mental processes must transcend the presence or absence of those processes. When we carefully attend to their comings and goings, we realize they do so in a kind of field that is more stable than they are. That field may be called *awareness*, our ability to recognize and react to stimuli. Still, our personal awareness itself shifts and slides in one direction or another, waxes and wanes, and even seems to totally disappear at times, such as in dreamless sleep or coma, and reappear, seemingly out of nowhere, when we awaken.

We now ask whether there is anything more real that gives rise to awareness. This question leads in the same direction Socrates points, which is through the soul or psyche into consciousness itself. Consciousness in this context is not limited to wakefulness, which is closer in meaning to *awareness*. Neither is it the opposite of unconsciousness, as we imply in common speech. Rather, consciousness has many potentials for degrees of awareness, wakefulness, and lucidity, including all the unconscious processes that shape our perceptions, create our dreams, and regulate our bodies, and even the state of complete emptiness. In this sense, consciousness is the essential field, or container, in which everything comes and goes that we typically associate with it. When speaking of consciousness in this way, some have capitalized the C to indicate that at this level it must be transcendent and even Divine. Mystically speaking, Consciousness is one, *the* One, mysteriously transcendent and undivided and yet immanently experiencing Its own creativity, and thus Itself through countless individual perspectives in space and time and with varying degrees of lucidity. But what is necessary to become lucid and realize Consciousness in this way?

Plato regards the truest nature of things to remain hidden even from dianoia, the process of discursive reasoning that Socrates has mastered; lucidity requires more than that. Socrates' himself honors that limitation when he indicates that he still only partially knows the truth of himself. To know the highest truths on the way of oneness, Plato says we must move into the upper and longest segment of the line, labeled *Noesis,* which we may call "direct intuition." As noted in Chapter 2, we are not using the word *intuition* in its common sense of an assumption based on superficial observations, which belongs much further down the divided line. The word *intuition* literally means to "look or see into," just as etymology indicates for the core meaning of *speculation.* In terms of noesis, it means to be *directly aware* of something, even more aware than we are through the limited ranges of our physical senses. For example, you are aware of your mind, therefore you know you exist. You do not need to look into a mirror, hear your voice, or argue or analyze yourself into that knowledge, and you do not need anyone else to confirm it. It is not a theory or an abstraction, but is immediate, undeniable, and self-evident.

There is more to be directly known. It can happen when we have exercised dianoia to the extent that our reasoning suggests the reality of something we have not perceived with the senses, yet which our reasoning cannot fully explain. Consider that moment of mysterious conviction experienced by scientists and mathematicians when all their work points toward a solution to their problem, and they have hypotheses and theories about it, yet that solution remains unknown and elusive. More relevant to our present reflections, consider the profound depth reached by the mystics of all religions when they realize all their emotions, images, and words fail to account for the whole truth of anything worthy of the name *God* or *Ultimate Reality.* It is then in moments of silent surrender to the Ineffable that we may be receptive enough to experience noesis, direct intuition, contributing something like the missing piece of a puzzle. Such an illumination confers a knowing our reason alone cannot attain, but which reason has prepared us to recognize and meaningfully unfold.

The ancient sources of wisdom urge us to understand that our thoughts and feelings are always veils on the deeper mysterious truths of things. We must part those veils by contemplatively opening our hearts and minds to Consciousness Itself, uncluttered, unmasked, and unfettered by our thoughts and feelings, to directly encounter *That* which thinks and feels. In such a meditative state, we *receive* the enlightenment of noesis more than we make it happen. The deeper, archetypal truths of things reveal themselves to us, and it then becomes our task to find the words, images, and feelings that best reflect them, even though we know those tools will be inadequate.

In Plato's Allegory of the Cave, he asserts that the visible world of common sense is like a cave, with a few people who realize there is more to their existence than the fleeting shadows on the wall that were once the sole objects of their attention. They begin the challenging ascent out of the cave of opinion and common sense toward the light of day, perhaps even to directly look upon the beauty and glory of the sun, the Form of the Good. Thus, allegorically, they follow the way of oneness into the Intelligible Realm and learn the truths of things there. He further says that when those people return to the cave and try to explain what they know, it often sounds confused and nonsensical to the cave dwellers. Their words can seem to contradict or even attack common sense. Furthermore, they cannot avoid sounding self-contradictory, if for no other reason than it is paradoxical to speak of the infinite with finite terms, or to describe the wholeness and oneness of all things with the limited dualities inherent to human language. There is, after all, an inescapable absurdity in speaking of the Ineffable. That is why the greatest teachers of philosophy and spirituality are concerned with showing us a way out of the cave, a practical path to enlightenment about Consciousness Itself, rather than merely giving us rules of behavior and doctrines about what to think and believe.

There is something else significant in Plato's account of those who come back to the cave, which is that they *do* come back. While the transcendent knowledge of truth is the initiated philosopher's highest aim, it is not the final objective. One of the truths such a seeker must eventually come to know is that the various levels of existence are interconnected, each a part of the one unifying truth that interpenetrates and encompasses the wholeness of all. Likewise, all souls are intertwined in the Mystic Tie. It would be a denial of that truth, it would be a heinous lie, to attempt to completely detach oneself from the Visible Realm and our brothers and sisters who have not yet learned to cross its boundaries. Furthermore, to attempt to do nothing but continually seek noesis in contemplation of our true self would, ironically, be a refusal to accept part of the complete truth of our existence, and thus put us at odds with others and our own wholeness. Accordingly, our tradition's way of oneness not only leads the contemplative Mason to view with reverence and admiration the glorious works of creation and inspires one with the most exalted ideas of the perfections of the divine Creator, but it also admonishes us to extend our kind offices to all and to let our inspirations guide us to be loving builders of wisdom, strength, and beauty in this world. Enlightened Master Masons are internally compelled to do so because they realize that the mysteries of the Divine and of existence are present here and now, and that *you* are the mysteries, just as they are.

To close, here is a contemplative poem related to the theme of the Great Mystery expressing itself in each of us.

ARTFULLY SHINING EYES

The Divine Mind lurks playfully

Behind the props and scenery

Of this enthralling mystery,

Like a shy child boldly giving

Spontaneous living voices

To a host of cherished dolls and puppets,

Freely exploring the limits

Of relationship and creativity.

How magical, then, the moments

Of silent mystical wonder,

When the face of a beloved is turning

To ponder the One who supplies its life,

And the One finds its very own light,

Transcendent, yet manifestly burning,

Within those artfully shining eyes.

CHAPTER FOUR
TO KNOW THYSELF IS TO LOVE THYSELF

To know anything as completely as possible, one must intentionally love it, which is to say one must fully welcome and accept
it as it is and then become one with it. As we saw in the previous
chapter, the Ancient Mysteries and their contemporary reflection in
Masonry challenge us to know ourselves in the deepest and most
complete way. Yet, as is also evident from our recent reflections, we
must admit that most of us are, to some extent, ignorant of ourselves
and even in conflict with ourselves. This chapter therefore delves
deeper into the inner work of lovingly bringing ourselves to a greater

state of wholeness and harmony, and thereby enabling us to more fully realize the Mystic Tie.

Defining Self

The term *self* is used in different ways. In fact, substantial confusion and disagreement can happen between people communicating with each other using the word *self*. Such troubles often occur simply because the various parties do not realize they are using *self* in significantly different ways. The same problems arise with other words like *psyche, soul, ego,* and even *mind*. So, we should begin by establishing what is meant by *self* in this book.

In the present text, *self, soul,* and *psyche* are practically interchangeable. These terms here refer to the whole being of an individual human – physical, emotional, intellectual, spiritual – and not any single part or function of the whole. It may also be helpful to consider that the term *ego* does not equate with *self*. *Ego* instead describes certain aspects of the self and is most notably connected with the illusion of separateness.

Self-Image

The *self-image* includes the self-concept and is one's sense of who one is as an individual human being. By analogy, the self-image is to the self as a photo of your body is to your actual body; one is only a limited representation or reflection of the other. This distinction is important because when we speak in terms of *myself, me,* or *I*, we are usually actually referring to the self-image rather than the self, which is to say one is speaking about parts of the whole self as perceived by other parts. In fact, we so rarely speak of the whole self that we sometimes highlight doing so by emphasizing the word *whole*.

This conflation of the self with the self-image is evidence that most of us live in a pervasive state of fragmentation, self-deception, and confusion about our own being. In this confusion, habitually thinking and speaking of the self-image as if it is the whole self, we compound our lack of lucidity and the illusion of separation from the One and All. We can also maintain it because we sense the need to protect the self-image from realities or potentialities within the self that we regard as unacceptable in some way. This is where the idea of the ego becomes more relevant. The theory of *ego defense mechanisms* is based upon this dynamic of protecting the self-image, and these mechanisms are highly worthy of anyone's study. The Jungian concept of the psychological *Shadow* is also relevant, and it is addressed in greater depth later.

THE MYSTERY OF SELF

When we meditate carefully on the self, it becomes clear that we lack complete awareness of it. The many autonomous functions of our physical organs are themselves sufficient evidence that there are parts and processes frequently hidden within the self. Further and perhaps even more powerful evidence of self-mystery is found with the experience of intuitive insight, the storage and recall of memories, the unexpected upwelling of emotions, and the unpredictable and often puzzling content of our dreams. These things reveal the existence of *subconscious* or *unconscious* levels of mind. So it is that, even when we understand the distinction between the self and the self-image, we cannot think, speak, or write about the self with complete knowledge and understanding.

We are often unaware of the mystery of the self, perhaps at times even blissfully so, but it is an inescapable fact. Sometimes this ignorance seems to loom around us, filled with foreboding uncertainties. In trying to make sense of ourselves, it can feel like standing on the edge of an abyss in complete darkness, where any movement at all might send us falling to our doom. Yet, as we previously considered, the doom that we fear is often only the loss of our cherished illusions.

Entering the mystery of the self is therefore essential to liberation from some of the falseness and limitations of the self-image. It is part of the path of lucidity and freedom in realizing and actualizing more of our unfathomable potentials. Out of this mystery emerges the amazing light of creativity we express in our love of play, romance, philosophy, art, science, and spirituality.

According to those who have penetrated most deeply into the mystery of the self, one of its potentials is the realization of mystical union, or directly encountering and more intentionally harmonizing with the Mystic Tie. At first, one may make the rational observation that, simply in its mysteriousness, the human self is like all of reality. For there is some degree of mystery in everything. Likewise, whatever it is we mean by the word *God*, we must acknowledge that it is significantly interwoven with our sense of the most profound mysteries. In this regard, we can gain a special appreciation for what it means to be created in the image of God; being mysterious is something that both the self and God have in common!

Pondering this commonality can lead us to consider that there might be more to it than a parallel of two different mysteries. It is natural for us to wonder if self and God might be interwoven in a way that is beyond complete comprehension. As we saw in previous chapters, those who have developed mystical realization insist that such an intersection is real, that it is the universally shared omnipresent point of reality within the circle of all creation; it is the eternal spiritual heart of the Cosmic Self and all the temporal individual selves It begets, contains, and infuses. There, in that point, we can discover the unity among self-love, love of others, and love of the One and All, the whole oneness of Divine Love manifesting in its countless forms.

Approaching Self-Love

Many religions have their share of believers who insist that the most virtuous life is only achieved through self-denial, self-criticism, and even self-punishment. Even outside of religion some of these attitudes are often regarded as necessary for virtuous self-discipline. For many of us, that conditioning manifests as nagging and belittling ourselves for our shortcomings and mistakes, often harshly critiquing our successes and minimizing our talents. With some people, things can be much worse, including extreme self-imposed austerities, self-loathing, even intentional self-torture, including desires and actions taken for literal self-annihilation.

We must acknowledge that many respected religious leaders seem to have spoken of self-love as a vice. For example, Saint Ignatius of Loyola said:

> *Experience proves that in this life peace and satisfaction are had, not by the listless but by those who are fervent in God's service. And rightly so. For in their effort to overcome themselves and to rid themselves of self-love, they rid themselves of the roots of all passion and unrest.*

Statements like this are, in part, based upon the truthful realization that we are shortsighted, ignorant creatures who are often our own worst enemies, and upon the fact that we must sometimes submit to painful ordeals to experience genuine insight, healing, and growth. Yet, it is a sad irony that these truths are frequently interwoven with the belief that we must be consistently cruel and combative with ourselves to serve God better or to be more acceptable to God. So it is that many of us think, feel, and act as if we should continually be our own sado-masochistic interrogators, judges, and prison guards. It seems as if we must do so to demonstrate how terribly aware we are of our unworthiness, to keep ourselves out of trouble, and to exact from ourselves some degree of the retribution that we fear we deserve.

Noteworthy problems are inherent with such notions. To begin with, any attempt by the self to restrain or attack anything within the self is by necessity an act of self-assertion. It is simply delusional to convince ourselves that we are overcoming the self by our own effort, for it is the self that executes that very effort. There can thus be no self-denial in any complete sense, but only denial of one part of the self by another. There is also significant irony in the assumption that we have the power to make ourselves "better" through rejection and violence. In effect, we complicate the illusion of separation by habitually attacking some parts of ourselves with others, and we thereby ironically sanction aggressive harmfulness as the central means to peace and harmony – an inherently incongruous and misleading formula. This irrationality and embrace of hostility then fuels further self-deceptions, and the more we deceive ourselves the more likely we are to do harm to ourselves in other ways.

Unfortunately, these ills cannot simply be contained within us. The more one succumbs to self-deception, self-fragmentation, and other forms of self-harm, the less able one is to be a lucid presence of wholeness, harmony, and love in this world. In the end, the self-neglect and self-abuse that are confused with self-discipline position us to contribute more to the ills of the world. There is hardly any of this that can rightly be called virtuous, mystical, or free from "the roots of all passion and unrest."

By now, it should be apparent that when speaking of self-love, we are speaking of neither narcissistic obsession with our self-image nor selfish excess at the expense of others, nor are we denying the value of genuine humility. These mistakes would be the other side of the coin for a fragmented psyche. Spoiling the ego with over-indulgence, irrational positivity, or arrogance is typically an attempt at sugarcoating deep-seated dissatisfaction and despair. The fragmentation resulting from the refusal to face the uncomfortable truths of oneself may then be projected onto others, even the entire world, as if the biggest problems and solutions in our lives are "out there." A brooding distrust can then manifest in pendulum swings between demonizing and angelizing others, while between those poles may be a false laissez-faire detachment from concerns about anything, if not a seemingly nihilistic avoidance of any intentional valuing in life.

The ways we do and do not love ourselves shape the ways that we do and do not love others; to a significant degree, we cannot help but love others as we love ourselves, for better or worse. This view is more than a rationally sound appreciation of self-love; it draws attention to the deep psychological dynamics by which one's moral character in the world is formed. By analogy, consider that people who starve the body of food and water eventually become unable to serve others food and water. Thankfully, the more we practice genuinely loving awareness, acceptance, understanding, compassion, forgiveness, and caring for ourselves, the more able we are to freely do the same for others. In the 13th century, the Christian theologian Thomas Aquinas expressed the essential wisdom of authentic self-love very simply and directly: "Well-ordered self-love, whereby man desires a fitting good for himself, is right and natural."

If our highest calling as Masons is to realize greater lucidity in unity, wholeness, and harmony with the Mystic Tie, then insights like these beg us to remember that the place most immediately present and constantly available for such work is within oneself. Furthermore, if we are also inclined to trust the scriptures and mystics claiming that God is love, and that to be loving is to know God, then the most immediately present and constantly available way of knowing God would be through loving one's whole mysterious self. The self is an expression of Ultimate Reality, or said another way, a child of God, and so it simply deserves to be treated with respect, care, and compassion, perhaps especially by itself. Since the self as defined here includes the physical body, then caring for its health and fitness is a very important part of self-love, making oneself a more effective instrument of the Great Architect. You are highly encouraged to give these matters due attention, but our present focus is on the more contemplative dimensions of self-love.

MYSTICAL PRAYER

Masonry teaches that all noble work should begin with prayer, and thus it is our first formal practice of mystical love, one which is simultaneously an act of love for God and for self. Prayer can be defined in many ways, but perhaps the most succinct and appropriate way for our purposes is that prayer is the attempt to intentionally communicate with the Divine, with Ultimate Reality, the One. That attempt is mystical in character when it is done with faith and understanding, if not actual knowledge, that the Divine is within you and that you are part of it. Mystical prayer therefore classically includes deep relaxation and silently opening to the presence of God, wordlessly welcoming Deity's manifestation within oneself in that very moment, in whatever way it may be present, such as the silence itself.

Even so, as mystics, we do not deny that our personalities are less than the whole of ourselves or that they remain somewhat mired in the illusion of separation. These conditions make it natural for many of us to also continue relating to the Divine as another personal being. Thankfully, we can regard the Mystic Tie as immediately present within our internal lodge, that which is most real about us, while we also recognize the appeal and value of relating to God as other. The appeal and value are largely emotional, involving feelings like awe, wonder, humility, reverence, gratitude, and joy. Among other things, such powerful emotions can break down the illusory walls of the self-separating ego through acknowledgement of life's overwhelming mystery and grandeur. Those walls must fall to reveal very deep parts of ourselves that cannot be fully grasped by our rational thoughts. Thus, we are enabled to be more aware and understanding of the wholeness of self, including the self's oneness with the Divine. The instinctive need to do such things is one reason humans enjoy creating and experiencing inspirational poetry and music. Prayer is in that same category of artistry.

To enact self-love through mystical prayer, it should ideally be engaged as a daily practice on the way of oneness. Indeed, you are encouraged to establish routine times every day. You are also welcome to use any traditional prayer that seems mystical to you, compose your own for repeated use, offer extemporaneous prayers, or alternate or combine these options as you wish. The following guidelines are provided for reference in performing mystical prayer and in composing or searching for prayers. Some elements can be rearranged or even omitted. Think of them more as beneficial conditions for mystical prayer rather than a rigid set of steps.

1. As noted, mystical prayer can be grounded in an attitude consisting of one or more appropriate feelings – awe, wonder, humility, reverence, gratitude, and joy. You can call upon the feelings by first becoming still and quiet, and then remembering and responding to the mystery of being and the vastness and grandeur of creation. Give yourself plenty of time to relax your body and breathe slowly, deeply, and peacefully. Doing so lays the best possible foundation for the other elements of mystical prayer.

2. Lovingly address the Divine, either silently or aloud. This is an excellent place to connect Masonic mysticism with your personal religion by using whatever name, title, or image of Deity is most meaningful to you.

3. Offer a statement of praise by succinctly expressing your highest concept of the Divine, or at least one thing you believe or know to be true about the Divine that enhances your sacred feelings. As part of a mystical prayer, this statement should include or be congruent with your faith in or knowledge of oneness.

4. Earnestly declare your heartfelt desire, intention, and hope for greater awareness, understanding, and manifestation of harmonious wholeness and oneness with the Divine.

5. Acknowledge that your personal awareness alone is not sufficient to realize your aspirations, that you need and welcome assistance such as inspiration, motivation, guidance, and support of various kinds.

6. Express your gratitude for the assistance you have received or are receiving, and your faith and hope for what you are yet to receive.

7. Affirm the limitations of your thoughts and feelings, and your openness to the Mystic Tie's mysterious presence within you, here and now.

8. Sit in silence, patiently attending to the present moment within yourself, with a focus on openness to oneness. Let go of all your thoughts, feelings, and perceptions, holding on to none as they may come and go. This focus can be facilitated by a word or short phrase, such as "one," "open," or "open to oneness," which you use to lovingly redirect yourself when distracted. This open and receptive part of the process is the core of mystical prayer and deserves the greatest portion of your time.

9. When you feel moved to end the prayer, do so in whatever manner seems reverently appropriate to you, such as saying "Amen" or "So mote it be," or bowing.

SHADOW WORK

In the practice of mindfulness, reflection, and attending to silence, we can become aware of how we are sometimes at odds with ourselves – thinking, feeling, and doing things that we believe we would rather not. The intention to see and accept as much of the truth about ourselves as possible and the humility to remember that we always have blind spots in ourselves leads us to better grasp and come to terms with the psychological Shadow. The Shadow is that part of ourselves created by our conditioning and conclusions that some parts or potentials within our nature are unacceptable or unallowable. In our contemplative moments, we can be more sensitive to the formation of the Shadow as our own inner critic says "no" to some things and "yes" to others in the ego's ongoing attempt to define the self-image in its preferred way.

The rejected things are relegated to the darkness behind our self-image, out of sight, but not entirely out of mind because they continue to exist within us. No matter how strongly we attempt to deny or banish whatever we regard as ugly, dangerous, weak, or otherwise undesirable, they remain, at least as hidden potentials. Furthermore, they eventually find ways to come to the surface of our lives, typically without our awareness until it is too late. That is when we surprise ourselves with an impulsive action or we look back in hindsight on clearly self-contradictory behaviors. These "ruffians" within us can do considerable damage to us and our relationships if we merely turn our backs on them, pretending they are not lurking in the dark places of our personal temples. To love ourselves and know wholeness and harmony within self as fully as possible, we must get accustomed to keeping an eye on the Shadow.

Some things within the Shadow are not very ugly or dangerous at all. Instead, they are simply things we have regarded as unattainable or less desirable in some way. For instance, consider a boy who grows up in a family where artistic self-expression is chauvinistically regarded as "girly," and so, in his desire to be masculine, he teaches himself to disregard his natural and healthy desire to dance. Another example might be someone who experienced early struggles with mathematics due to a poor teacher, but rather than realizing the truth of inadequate instruction, the person came to falsely believe they lacked the capacity to do well in mathematics. Yet another example is that of a child who has been raised in a family where any overt expression of sadness is judged as weak and disgusting. Thus, the individual learns to swallow sadness to the extent that they are no longer aware of its presence. So, rather than any normal sadness being managed and expressed in healthy ways, it instead unconsciously manifests through other possibilities like pollyannaish attitudes, avoidance, and denial of naturally saddening situations, a cold and brittle "toughness," or insensitivity and even hostility to the sadness of others. There are countless ways like these that each of us has pushed things into the Shadow that could otherwise be beneficial to ourselves and others.

It is not necessary or even advisable to try to fully actualize everything in the Shadow, but rather to try to see, understand, and integrate as much as possible. In this context, to *integrate* means to first recognize that there are always elements of wisdom, strength, and beauty within those things we are tempted to reject, and to then welcome those elements as capable of being employed for constructive, life-affirming and joyous purposes. To do so is to move toward greater wholeness, an important aspect of the way of oneness.

As an analogy for avoiding versus integrating aspects of the Shadow, consider the folly in rejecting fire in all forms because of its potentials for destruction and creating pain. That folly is just as great as brazenly ignoring those potentials and indiscriminately playing with fire. We must exercise awareness, acceptance, and comprehension of fire's negative potentials if we are to understand and manifest its positive potentials. Among other things, fire can be an analogy for anger, an emotion that can indeed be very harmful and which many people have become habituated to denying and suppressing within the Shadow until it explodes into uncontrolled and often misdirected rage. Anger is also a perfectly natural emotion and one with very healthy potentials if we practice awareness, understanding, and thoughtful manifestations of it. There are many other things within us besides anger for which this analogy can be quite informative, including sexual desire.

Because Shadow work includes accepting the less pleasant and polite things about ourselves, some people mistakenly seem to think it is an excuse to let their "inner jerks" come out. Shadow work is not a license to stop being kind, courteous, caring, and thoughtful in what one says and does, and to instead become rude, tactless, insensitive, and impulsive. Such attitudes tend to foster feelings of otherness and separation instead of facilitating realization of unity, wholeness, and harmony. Even so, for many people Shadow work includes undoing some of their conditioning to please others by sacrificing their own authenticity, integrity, and creativity. Many of us have been trained to be people-pleasers to the extent that we automatically shut off things in us that might be helpful, even if a little discomforting for others. Successfully resolving such tendencies is a good development in self-love, and it can also be a tricky one in which mistakes are likely to happen, including pendulum swings of over-compensation. Still, none of this is a justification for being intentionally offensive and uncaring.

In any case, peering into the darkness behind the self-image can be scary, and it can be challenging and painful, but there is no substitute for such inner work. The spiritualized ego that speaks *only* in grand glowing terms of light, love, and bliss is simultaneously casting a large heavy Shadow. One may not only be doing so for oneself, but in the process also encouraging others to do likewise, and thereby propagating the tendency to fragment ourselves and even foolishly embrace narcissism rather than genuine transformation. We not only owe it to ourselves to do Shadow work, but also to each other.

So, beyond practicing self-awareness and self-acceptance in our inner work, how do we begin more intentionally welcoming parts of ourselves out of the Shadow and into the light of a more whole complete self-awareness? One approach to revealing the Shadow is to catch ourselves speaking or thinking in ways that would exclude from ourselves things we witness in others, whether desirable or not. Clues include compulsively making judgmental statements about another's mistakes or foibles, or self-deprecation while observing another's successes or talents. In either case, the insinuation, if not overt declaration, is "That's not me!" Other tip-offs are thoughts or statements like, "I just don't have that in me," "I could never do that," "Who could possibly do/say/think/want such a thing?" or "That is totally unacceptable." Also consider attitudes of annoyance or disgust with songs, images, characters, and other elements of art and popular culture; these can also be reflections of things in ourselves that we would rather not face. When we notice ourselves having any of these reactions, we can pause to sincerely acknowledge that we might indeed have the perceived elements somewhere within us. Once the acknowledgment is made, then a more thorough self-examination may shed further light.

As previously noted, the Shadow significantly involves the personal unconscious and is therefore not entirely within sight of personal awareness. So, for people who recall their dreams, a potentially powerful means for Shadow work is to remember that everything experienced in a dream is produced through interaction of personal awareness with the unconscious mind. Thus, any dream element that you regard as too foreign, frightening, bizarre, painful, disgusting, or even too talented, beautiful, or angelic for you to personally identify with, is still most likely based on potentials you can find within yourself. Taking such things into meditation, journaling, and dialoging about them with others are three ways to significantly enhance the insight that can come from your dreams.

Shadow work is one of the keys to unlocking the deepest self-knowledge and most authentic self-actualization we can manage. Without it, our efforts at transformation may be little more than narcissistic attempts by our egos to polish the false idols of themselves, no matter how wise, strong, and beautiful they might appear. Still, the people most adept at doing this work know the whole self remains mysterious, and that the process of its flowering and transformation is not, and cannot be, determined only by what one thinks and attends to. Realizing this truth, such persons often seem to blend a sense of lighthearted humor with profound respect for the complexity and mysteries of their own being. This practice also tends to foster a deeper sense of kinship and compassion for others, no matter where they might be with regard to understanding and engaging any of these dynamics. The more one knows and integrates the Shadow, which includes embracing the mystery of things beyond our awareness and control, the more one sees oneself in others and others in oneself, including the mysteries we all are to ourselves and each other. This greater level of acceptance in every direction is intimately connected with a broader, deeper, and more loving embrace of unity, wholeness, and harmony.

SELF-LOVE IN ATTUNING WITH THE MYSTIC TIE

Many spiritual traditions and authorities assert that the most profound embrace of oneness within self is directly encountering Ultimate Reality resident there. To contemplatively open oneself to such a possibility is an act of self-love because the Divine is, in the language of the Builder's Art, both the cornerstone and the keystone of the self. Furthermore, even if one never knows the Absolute through the most complete dissolution of otherness, the prayerfully expressed desire for a more comprehensive communion can facilitate the development of greater wholeness and harmony among the various elements of the self.

Academics and scholars like R.C. Zaehner and Walter T. Stace refer to the focus on such an inward experience as *introverted mysticism*, distinguishing it from a concern with experiencing the Divine in or through things external to oneself, which is called *extroverted mysticism*. Theologians such as Valentin Tomberg have used the term *enstasy* to differentiate the experience of introverted mysticism from the more familiar ecstasies of extroverted spirituality. Robert K.C. Forman, a professor and author in the field of consciousness studies, refers to the most exceptional experience of enstasy as the *pure consciousness event*, echoing other mystics who have stated that Ultimate Reality, the Monad, or God, may be realized as the pristine essence of Consciousness Itself.

Forman's choice of the word *event* rather than *experience* is quite intentional. There is a logical problem with referring to total oneness as an "experience" because that implies the duality of (1) an experiencer and (2) that which is experienced. By analogy, when we look in the mirror at our own image, or even think about our own minds, what we experience is not fully immediate and direct. There is an objectification, an otherness, created by the perceptual process, a representation that we construct rather than unmediated, unmoderated, totally undifferentiated unification of the perceiver, the perceived, and the perception. It is for this reason that mystics who claim direct knowledge of oneness sometimes use terms like *event* or *state*, although these terms, even *oneness*, cannot avoid their own dualistic implications.

The quintessential knowledge, event, state, or experience of oneness, like the true name of Deity, is ineffable. Words and other symbols only metaphorically point toward it, or describe it by its effects, or indicate by negation what it is not. Consider the following excerpts from one mystic's attempt to communicate the oneness of total communion with the Divine and an explosive return to the duality of otherness, while also acknowledging the inadequacy of the chosen words:

THE INEFFABLE WHATNESS

[...]

My teacher asked,

"What do you see

when you close your eyes?"

"Whatever is in my imagination."

"What if you don't imagine anything?"

So, I closed my eyes, and...

What shall I call it now, after the fact?

Darkness, because there was no light?

Silence, because there were no sounds?

Emptiness, because there were no thoughts?

Nothingness, because there were no things?

Stillness, because there was no movement?

Timelessness, because there was no change?

There was no longer any 'me,'

neither memory nor anticipation,

but, there was... What?

Presence?

Perhaps, but if so,

then presence without context,

neither location nor duration.

Consciousness?

Perhaps, but if so,

then consciousness without process,

neither reflection nor projection.

Oneness?

Perhaps, but if so,

then oneness without dimension,

neither extension nor limitation.

Suddenly, a blast of golden amber light!

It filled the void like a flood of bright buzzing honey,

and with it an awareness without words

that "it" was "this,"

all of it,

all of this.

The unseen eye that saw it all

evolved into the unspoken "I,"

filled with the unthought knowledge

and the unevoked bliss

of being and becoming.

[...]

Then came the willing return

to ordinary wakefulness,

with the ineffable *Whatness*

of that mysterious non-imagining

as the point within the golden circle

of a lifetime of reflections.

There is another very profound and potentially troubling aspect to such an experience, state, or event, which is that we apparently cannot *make* it happen. It does not seem to simply be a matter of devotedly working at some set of practices that guarantee arriving at the supreme destination. One explanation for this conundrum is that dualistic consciousness cannot use dualistic means to arrive at oneness. Only *That* which transcends duality can dissolve all elements of the self into undifferentiated identification with *It*. (Even this statement has dualistic limitations!)

Evidence for this truth has been provided by seekers who have spent their lives in committed mystical practice, and then died before having received what they most desired. On the other hand, there have been persons who, with little or even no special practice, have reported knowledge consistent with the accounts of other mystics who have realized oneness with Ultimate Reality, the Absolute. Yet, it also appears to be the case that totally intimate realization of oneness does occur more often among those who devotedly practice disciplines with that aim. Some authorities therefore suggest it is better to regard mystical practices as *preparing* for a unitive mystical event rather than *producing* it. Another encouraging observation is that devoted practice can more predictably lead to degrees of greater lucidity in perceiving oneness through the veils of otherness. In other words, even without experiencing a totally unitive mystical event, it is possible to attain levels of awareness and understanding of oneness with the Mystic Tie that are significantly less clouded by the illusion of separation. Here is an attempt to describe and evoke a sense of intuitive lucidity about the immanence of the One within all:

WHO IS AWAKENING TO THE DREAM

Just now, the veils on this world are thin.

A teardrop is a gate to the Kingdom,

and streams crossing the current of time

flow out and return to the roots of the soul.

Another's words are echoes

from a thought not yet spoken,

and, like walking on the ceiling in a dream,

the mind awakens to see its own making,

feeling the unknowable expanse of itself,

the Dreamer who dreams of the one

who is awakening to the Dream.

There is, after all, value in mystical practices such as those already offered. We therefore turn our attention to an additional practice with the potential to further facilitate lucidity, and perhaps even open the way for a state of total communion with the Mystic Tie. This practice involves using the power of repetitive chant and imagery to help shift awareness more deeply into attunement with oneness. Chanting is well suited to this purpose because its recurring vibrations can have significant effects on the systems of the body, on the emotions, and on the intellect. It can facilitate relaxation, oxygenating the blood, pacifying the emotions, and focusing attention in a way that can free the mind from much of its usual chatter and distractibility. The repeated sound, word, or phrase (commonly denoted by the Sanskrit term *mantra*), and perhaps an accompanying image, often allude to if not literally express one's meditative intention.

There are many options, both traditional and innovative, for mantras and images to facilitate attuning with the Mystic Tie. The mantra presently offered is the Latin phrase *unum in omnia*, which means "one in all" and thus overtly addresses the way of oneness. Its subject and object of similar sounds also allude to the veils of duality – as above, so below – through which we may intuitively perceive the self's oneness with the Mystic Tie and which might even be parted to draw us directly into undifferentiated union with it. As a mantra addressing the Divine One and expressing your openness to communion, it is also a prayer of invocation.

While chanting this mantra, hold an image of the All-Seeing Eye in your brow. The mystical traditions of many cultures associate the brow with intuition, mystical insight, spiritual vision, and one's transcendent connection with the Divine. Master Masons might also make a meaningful connection with a certain *brow of a hill*. We apply this visualization at this location because it signifies the watchful presence of the Divine, which knows each of us from within, deeper, and more completely than we know ourselves. The image and mantra also express one's desire to more fully welcome and commune with the mysterious Divine essence of one's being, and thus "Know Thyself" in the deepest possible way. It is helpful to associate these tools with a profound sense of tranquility and intimate connectedness with the Absolute.

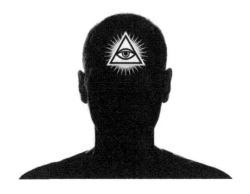

For this practice, it can be useful to set a timer for at least 20 minutes. An ideal time might be before sleep, as that is a time when we are naturally withdrawn from social life and preparing to let go of our personal waking state and sense of separateness. In any case, take a stable position for meditation, start the timer if you are using one, close your eyes and go through a process of relaxation and mystical prayer, just as introduced earlier in this chapter. Then proceed through these steps:

1. After attaining deep relaxation and peaceful breathing, as you attend to the silence, recognize that beyond the veil of your perception of the silence is the mysterious source of everything that flows into the silence, the enigmatic ground to which everything returns, and the inscrutable essence of it all, including the silence and that which perceives within the silence.

2. Recall that this mysterious, enigmatic, and inscrutable One is the Mystic Tie and facilitate your focus upon it by chanting the mantra *unum in omnia* and visualizing the All-Seeing Eye in your brow, glowing with a white aura. Each repetition should extend throughout a long slow exhalation, giving approximately equal time to the sound of each vowel and consonant. If circumstances allow, the chant should be pronounced loudly enough to feel its vibrations in the palette and brow. A higher pitch and nasal quality in your voice can aid with the sensation. If you are concerned about privacy or disturbing others, it can be performed quietly, as a whisper or even silently.

3. As you repeat the mantra, allow your focus upon it and the image of the All-Seeing Eye, and feelings of tranquil connectedness, to overcome all other mental activity as much as possible. Do your

best to ignore any other imagery that might arise. Let attending to the immediate experience of the mantra and image take precedence over thinking about it and its meanings or effects. Try to not let yourself be distracted by the associations formed by your personal consciousness or the unconscious mind.

4. After several repetitions, allow the mantra to shift to an entirely internal repetition, releasing your attention on the breath to focus as exclusively as possible on the mantra and All-Seeing Eye in your brow. In this practice it is possible to arrive at an experience that has sometimes been described as becoming the mantra or the mantra repeating itself.

5. In time, it may be possible for the mantra and image to fall away as awareness naturally transitions into a state of transcendence beyond ordinary mental activity, one far less encumbered by sensations, feelings, images, or concepts. This state might quickly pass, or it could linger. In either case, with its passing, mental phenomena – like sensory perceptions, emotions, words, or images – may once again capture a bit of attention. Whenever you become aware of such changes, simply return to the internal repetition of the mantra with attention centered on the All-Seeing Eye in the brow as often and for as long as necessary.

6. When you are ready to stop or the timer has gone off, reground yourself through attending to each of your physical senses, one after another, ending with sight as you open your eyes. Take a moment to note the effects of the meditation before proceeding with other activities.

Note that a session has gone well and been beneficial even if the entire time in step 5 was spent internally repeating the mantra and visualizing the image. Not everything about this practice is within our personal control. We should therefore be cautious about establishing narrow or rigid expectations for the practice, which may only stimulate frustration and disappointment. Still, with long-term routine practice, it is generally true that some of the deeper potentials of this meditation can more consistently manifest. The mantra and image can also be recalled and silently repeated at various times throughout one's day to reconnect in some measure with awareness of unity. In any case, the practice is meant to be easy, and in one sense it is perfectly true that it is about nothing more than repeating the mantra and visualizing the image as an act of love for oneself and the Ultimate Reality that is one's essence.

CONCLUSION

In this chapter we have emphasized the importance of self-love to the way of oneness and mystical realization, especially through self-awareness and self-acceptance. Given that we are working with the perspective that everything is an expression of the Absolute, then to be unloving to any aspect of oneself is to neglect and perhaps even abuse part of the One's wholeness. Through loving integration of one's inner ruffians, they become transformed from obstacles to instruments by which we may more intentionally, compassionately, and harmoniously participate with others in the Mystic Tie. By communing with the Divine essence of ourselves, we more fully unite our various elements and align them in oneness with Ultimate Reality. These themes and other subtleties of mystical self-love are reflected in this poem:

DEEP WITHIN THE WELL OF THIS HEART

Deep within the well of this heart,

sliding down in the silent darkness,

sinking into the caverns of spirit,

I found You, beloved One,

the hidden waters,

a mighty rushing in the stillness.

There at Your edge,

where I might have plunged

and fulfilled the fantasy

of a supreme union,

I found instead

the fear of oblivion in You,

and upon this halting

I piled remorse and shame

for my self-judged unworthiness.

Still, I dipped a begging hand

into Your ceaseless current,

washed the tear-stained dust

from this mask of sadness

and sipped a drop of Your cool purity.

Such sweet wine You are,

beloved One,

for this single taste

bestowed an unimagined sobriety,

a joyous awakening to the memory

that this resistance to Your fullness

is among the greatest gifts from You.

In these depths,

all things left within me

that had seemed to interfere

with my dream of perfection

were revealed as channels

for a unique upwelling

of Your goodness.

You created me to be Your lover,

my Beloved.

By Your will we are two

who are nonetheless one.

Never let this be undone

so long as there are others in this world

who thirst for You.

CHAPTER FIVE
THE MYSTICISM OF FRATERNAL LOVE

While the practices described in the previous chapter are focused on the individual, it is also obvious that there are several points of connection to our relationships with others. As solitary and private as such inner work and mystical realization can be, they are not whole if we ignore the social dimensions of our being. We were created and have evolved as communal creatures, and our mystic quest must account for that fact.

In numerous ways, Masonry draws attention to the fact that we are social beings and that we benefit from embracing that truth. We are literally conceived in relationship, born into relationship, and our dependence on a nurturing relationship for our very survival is extraordinarily long compared to other species. Indeed, the science of human development has observed that without adequately healthy loving relationships, we cannot optimize our physical, emotional, and intellectual potentials. Furthermore, all of us eventually find ourselves in situations where our challenges and risks are greater than we can manage entirely on our own, and so it is natural for us to seek aid from others. As a parallel in Masonry, consider that every step from candidacy for initiation to being raised as a Master Mason requires a significant amount of willing assistance from others. The Craft is not a hermit's path! It teaches that the Builder's Art should be performed within a context of harmonious and mutually supportive relationships, and there are sound reasons for doing so.

The Christian mystic, Evelyn Underhill, began her answer to the question of a mystic's need for community thusly:

> *First and most obviously, it gives him a favourable environment. He must have an environment: he must be affected by it. That is a certainty in the case of any living thing; a certainty so obvious that it would be hardly worth stating were it not that those who talk about the mystic craving for solitude [...] seem often to ignore it. The idea of solitude in any complete sense is, of course, an illusion. We are bound, if we live at all, to accept the fact of a living world outside ourselves, to have social relations with something; and it only remains to decide what these relations shall be.*

On this theme, Zen teacher Norman Fischer recounts a tale from the *Meghiya Sutta* of the Pali text. The Buddha's disciple,

Meghiya, complained of his difficulty with practicing meditation in the solitude he had been granted after his insistent requests. The text says:

> *"Five things induce release of heart and lasting peace,"* the *Buddha told him. "First, a lovely intimacy with good friends. Second, virtuous conduct. Third, frequent conversation that inspires and encourages practice. Fourth, diligence, energy, and enthusiasm for the good. And fifth, insight into impermanence."*

Then, for Meghiya's further benefit and to cement the argument, the Buddha goes through the list again, this time preceding each of the other items with the first: "When there is a lovely intimacy between friends, *then* there is virtuous conduct," et cetera. In other words, according to the Buddha, friendship is the most crucial element in the spiritual quest. Everything else naturally flows from it. Similarly, the Sufi master al-Gazzali taught that mystics need a community in which they mutually embrace eight duties to each other: material aid, personal support, respect, praise and attention, forgiveness, prayer, loyalty, and relief from discomfort. It is likewise integral to the Builder's Art that we both give and receive support of various kinds, thereby enabling each other to become more virtuous, enlightened, and whole individuals with healthy, harmonious, meaningful relationships.

From a mystical perspective, it makes perfect sense that Masonry's Principal Tenets are Brotherly Love, Relief, and Truth, and it is worthwhile to carefully examine what our rituals and monitors say about them, listening for resonances with the words of those mystics just reviewed.

Brotherly Love

By the exercise of Brotherly Love, we are taught to regard the whole human species as one family—the high, the low, the rich, the poor—who, as created by one Almighty Parent, and inhabitants of the same planet, are to aid, support, and protect each other. On this principle, Masonry unites men of every country, sect, and opinion, and conciliates true friendship among those who might otherwise have remained at a perpetual distance.

Brotherly Love or Friendship is regarded by Freemasons as the strong cement of the Order; without this high moral virtue, the Fraternity would soon cease to exist. By Brotherly Love, we are to understand that generous principle of the soul which regards the human species as one family, created by an All-wise Being, and placed on this globe for the mutual assistance of each other. The man who is actuated by the pure principle of Brotherly Love, will not desert his friend when dangers threaten or misfortunes assail him. When he is calumniated, he will openly and boldly espouse his cause, and endeavor to remove the aspersion. When sickness or infirmity occasion him to be deserted by others, he will seize the opportunity, and redouble all the affectionate attentions which love suggests. No society can exist for any length of time, unless Brotherly Love prevail among its members. To "dwell together in unity," is the life and support of the great Masonic institution.

Relief

To relieve the distressed, is a duty incumbent on all men, but particularly on Masons, who are linked together by an indissoluble chain of sincere affection. To soothe the unhappy; to sympathize with their misfortunes; to compassionate their miseries, and to restore peace to their troubled minds, is the great aim we have in view. On this basis, we form our friendships and establish our connections.

Relief flows from brotherly love, as free, pure, and refreshing as the mountain air. It dries up the gushing fountains of grief, banishes want from the abode of a distressed brother, and pours the oil of joy into the wounded hearts of the widow and the orphan.

Truth

Truth is a divine attribute, and the foundation of every virtue. To be good and true, is the first lesson we are taught in Masonry. On this theme we contemplate, and by its dictates endeavor to regulate our conduct. Hence, while influenced by this principle, hypocrisy and deceit are unknown among us; sincerity and plain dealing distinguish us; and the heart and the tongue join in promoting each other's welfare, and rejoicing in each other's prosperity.

Truth is the foundation of all Masonic virtues; it is one of our grand principles; for to be good men and true, is a part of the first lesson we are taught; and at the commencement of our freedom we are exhorted to be fervent and zealous in the pursuit of truth and goodness. It is not sufficient that we walk in the light, unless we do so in the truth also. All hypocrisy and deceit must be banished from among us. Sincerity and plain dealing complete the harmony of a Lodge, and render us acceptable in the sight of Him unto whom all hearts are open, all desires known, and from whom no secrets are hid. There is a charm in truth, which draws and attracts the mind continually towards it. The more we discover, the more we desire; and the great reward is wisdom, virtue, and happiness. This is an edifice founded on a rock, which malice cannot shake or time destroy.

Brotherly Love, Relief, and Truth encompass the Masonic view of harmonious spiritual companionship and friendship. As has been noted by mystical authorities of diverse traditions, within such relationships and the sacred spaces created to nurture them, we have opportunities to practice and develop the virtues that facilitate our individual and collective wellness. In doing so, we assist each other in preparing our souls to receive mystical enlightenment, and thus to also manifest it more completely in harmonious wholeness with others.

Among the various virtues of our tradition, there is one that is fundamental to our fraternal culture, yet it is not highlighted in our ritual quite like others, and that is *toleration.* In a Masonic sense, toleration is the practice of not actively disregarding, opposing, resisting, or excluding people because of their religious or political opinions, beliefs, or practices. As discussed in Chapter 3, we all have attitudes and elements of lifestyle that are largely expressions of cultural factors as they intersect within us. Even if we regard ourselves as careful thinkers who have developed well-researched and thoroughly considered positions, we can still be powerfully affected by confirmation bias, logical fallacies, cognitive distortions, ego defense mechanisms, unconscious fears, desires, and conflicts, and plain ignorance. Because of these factors, the same material facts can be understood quite differently by different people, and the divergences are only multiplied when we enter matters as fluid as politics, religion, and art, to name but a few. If we are practicing the kind of loving self-awareness described in the previous chapter, then we know such things are true of us and that it does no good to exercise any hostility toward ourselves about them. We should therefore also know that we are not in any justifiable position to deny others the right to also be struggling with their own self-mystery, conditioning, egos, and Shadows on the quest for more light. In a very real sense, everyone on this planet is doing the best they can in each moment, given their level of awareness and understanding in that moment. Toleration is the virtue by which we extend to others the latitude for error, learning, and growth without which none of us could have or might yet become wiser, stronger, or more beautiful souls. Toleration also determines the degree to which we can apply the Master Mason's Trowel and find the common ground upon which as many as possible can best agree and work together.

As a fraternal virtue, toleration is the baseline minimum degree of Brotherly Love, Relief, and Truth that we have to offer anyone, whether members of our Fraternity or not. Brotherly Love is expressed in the simple caring and kindness of this virtue. Relief manifests to the extent that people can quite literally feel relieved that they are being respectfully met on the level and welcomed with dignity despite differences that might have otherwise marked them to be scorned as inferiors, feared as threats, or attacked as enemies. And Truth undergirds all of this in compassionate acknowledgment of the universal human struggles with darkness and light, but also in realization of the Mystic Tie that unites all regardless of the illusion of separation.

To be clear, like all true virtues, toleration is in the middle ground between extremes. Healthy toleration is neither too broad nor too narrow, neither too lax nor too strict. So, we observe the practice of "guarding the West Gate," for example. Toleration has due bounds, and it does not dispense with responsibility or account-ability for one's mistakes, especially when they contribute to suffering for others. Here is where we naturally turn to the Craft's tradition of whispering good counsel and to our work of developing the other virtues. So, in the following paragraphs, we more carefully contem-plate how the virtues of Masonry, specifically the Four Cardinal and Three Theological Virtues, are interwoven with our Principal Tenets and enable us to follow the way of oneness and participate in frater-nal manifestations of the Mystic Tie more fully.

THE LADDER OF THE PRINCIPAL TENETS & THE MYSTICAL POTENTIAL OF THE VIRTUES

Virtue hardly gets the attention it deserves in contemporary society, yet we live in an age filled with regulations and ethical standards that specify what is and is not acceptable conduct for a given occupation or environment. While sometimes scantly referencing virtuous principles, these codes are largely driven by and focused on matters of civil and criminal liability, rather than being aimed at providing means of harmonizing one's heart and mind with the divine ideals of wholeness and oneness. In fact, the very notion of a commitment to virtue is often laughed off as prudish and naïve, or worse, suspiciously regarded as a subterfuge designed to mask nefarious intentions.

Indeed, we too often speak as if human beings are essentially bitter, corrupt, and vile at the core. We use phrases like "how you *really* feel" or "what you *really* think" to imply that the unpleasantness someone chooses to keep private is in fact the central truth of who they are, how they view the world, and what they want in life. Such a negative attitude is a sickness that modern psychology has only recently begun to understand and address. Research is showing that chronic cynicism, pessimism, and suspicion not only form unrealistic and unhealthy mental and behavioral habits, but also lead to chemical and even structural changes in our brains and other organs that are harmful to our personal and social well-being. From a mystical perspective, these attitudes and actions are mechanisms that reinforce the illusions of separation and keep us from knowing and enjoying unity with God and harmony with each other. In Masonic language, they are vices that impede our ability to experience and express the Principal Tenets of Brotherly Love, Relief, and Truth individually and collectively. We therefore now turn our attention to the Principal Tenets and virtues of Masonry to better engage them as means to realizing unity, wholeness, and harmony with the Mystic Tie.

The Principal Tenets can be categorized according to three capacities of the human being: (1) perceptual, (2) behavioral, and (3) emotional.[6] *Perceptual capacity* includes not only the ability to use our senses, but also our intellect in recognizing and understanding what we sense, and it is therefore most aligned with Truth. *Behavioral capacity* accounts for what we do, with all its elements of preparation, execution, and termination, which naturally corresponds with Relief. *Emotional capacity* accounts for the psychophysiological energies that move us to respond to our perceptions, the forces of feelings like attraction, repulsion, affection, animosity, joy, sadness, peace, anger, and so on. Brotherly Love associates with this capacity.

It is important to note that these capacities and tenets are interrelated aspects of a whole; they are constantly affecting each other, and one cannot be fully understood without reference to the others. For example, while Brotherly Love may be most immediately experienced through emotions like affection, it also has behavioral and perceptual aspects. Likewise, Truth, although most aligned with perception, is intimately connected with behavior and emotions.

To explore their interconnectedness, let us add a useful element of imagery to this contemplation, visualizing the Principal Tenets and corresponding capacities as the parts of a ladder. The two rails are Truth/perception on one side, and Brotherly Love/emotion on the other, with Relief/behavior being the rungs between them. The rails provide direction while the rungs connect them and offer a path of movement between them. As with an actual ladder, the strength,

6. This section is an adaptation of Dunning, Jr., C.R., "The Ladder of Relief: A Contemplation on Acting in Truth and Brotherly Love," in *Fraternal Review*, vol. 62, no. 10, Southern California Research Lodge, November 2021.

stability, and utility of this metaphorical ladder depends on each rail and rung being securely connected with the whole.

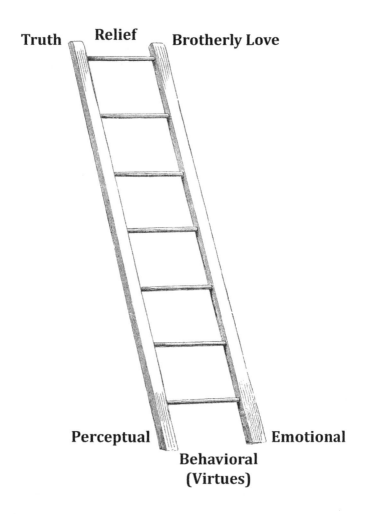

The perceptual rail of Truth represents the facts of the situation in which we consider offering Relief to another. It includes all the contributing factors, possibilities of what can be done, and the potential consequences of our actions or inaction. These perceptions also encompass the thoughts and feelings of the person we intend to help, as well as the strengths and weaknesses of our own abilities and resources. Mystically speaking, truth is what is actually real and really possible, and thus central to this tenet is maintaining a perspective on existence as the manifestation and revelation of the one Ultimate Reality.

The emotional rail of Brotherly Love corresponds to our feelings of care, concern, and the desire to help. It also consists of empathy, the ability to *feel with* the person we wish to assist. The intensity of feelings – the other's as well as our own – is relevant because it relates to our sense of urgency. In the mystical perspective, the emotions of Brotherly Love are energies we transmit and receive, and that move us (they are *e-motive*) to cherish and nurture joyous, harmonious interconnectedness with each other rather than succumb to the myriad kinds of discord and divisiveness that cloud the truth of our communion.

The behavioral rungs of ascent in performing Relief are not only about what we physically do, such as walking, shaking a hand, giving a hug, carrying something, typing, listening, or speaking. In this context, behavior also includes the internal cognitive actions of managing our thoughts and feelings, integrating our perceptions and our emotions, and making the decisions that lead to other actions. True mysticism is not just a collection of ideas about the nature of existence; it is a way of being and doing in which every dimension of one's existence is engaged in realizing unity, wholeness, and harmony.

Because the tenet of Relief is primarily focused on behavior, and wise behavior is virtuous, we now consider the rungs of Relief in correlation with the Four Cardinal and Three Theological Virtues. While this correlation could be arranged in various ways, the following set has a logical sequence and parallels the placement of the Theological Virtues found on many versions of the Entered Apprentice trestleboard.

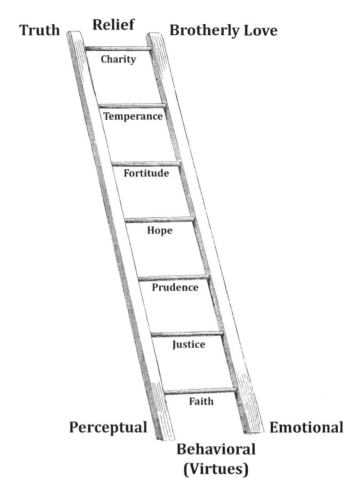

Faith is suggested as the first rung because, in its most basic sense, it is the trust needed to take any meaningful action in life. Regarding Relief, Faith is trust in ourselves, in the truthfulness of our perceptions, in the loving nature of our desires, and in our abilities to do something good. It is also trust in the immediate presence of the blessings and assistance of Deity. This first step requires our *faith-fullness* to act on our beliefs and values, or to "walk the walk, not just talk the talk" of working toward peace, harmony, and unity for others as well as ourselves.

The second rung, Justice, is not simply law and order, not merely about punishments to fit crimes. Justice is also about the basic level of care and concern for all others that makes for good relationships and a good society. This virtue serves the principle that it is simply inhumane, or unjust, to ignore another's suffering, which always includes the pains of separation and fragmentation. In Relief, Justice therefore entails acting not only with Faith but also with real motivation to acknowledge our interconnectedness and be actively caring even if it seems inconvenient or not personally profitable.

Prudence, the third step, is necessary to provide Relief wisely, and it should therefore always be grounded in the ever-present truth of the Mystic Tie. With that foundation, Prudence strives to comprehend the pertinent circumstances as clearly as possible, avoiding assumptions, seeking and listening to intuition and inspiration, and exercising forethought in determining what might and might not be genuinely helpful. This virtue therefore requires thoughtful communication, especially with those we offer Relief. While Prudence generally encourages circumspection, it also accounts for urgency and makes appropriate adjustments in cautiousness versus risk-taking.

Hope, based on prudent consideration, is an optimistic vision for a beneficial outcome from our efforts. It provides an inspiring reference point, a goal to guide one's actions. Hope also helps sustain and renew our motivation for Relief. Furthermore, the emotional energy of Hope is infectious and can lift the spirits of those we wish to serve and help rally others to our cause, thus revealing our underlying oneness in the natural tendency to resonate or harmonize with each other.

Fortitude is the commitment and perseverance necessary to follow through and keep working toward fulfillment of our hopeful intentions, even when things are more laborious, complicated, or time-consuming than expected. It is about continuing to serve one's vision despite resistance or unforeseen obstacles. Rather than always overpowering problems, Fortitude is also resilient and adaptable in finding skillful methods to make progress in providing Relief, even when the preferred means of doing so are unavailable. This virtue finds its deepest reserves in the Divine Presence, the ever-present life-force that feeds and sustains all.

Temperance means exercising moderation, avoiding doing too much or too little. It also promotes consistency, maintaining a harmonious, steady, and stable effort. The convictions of Faith, the motivation of Justice, the intentions of Prudence, the vision of Hope, and the zeal of Fortitude can all combine to make us passionate in performing Relief. Yet, even our most positive passions must be kept within due bounds lest they become either ineffectual or harmful. Among other things, Temperance helps keep the "cure" of Relief from being worse than the "disease" of whatever suffering we mean to address. In the mystical view, intemperance, no matter how motivated it is to reveal oneness, wholeness, and harmony, may instead re-veil them in even more deceptive and hurtful ways.

Charity, in its theological meaning, is unconditional universal love, not simply material generosity. It is love for others that reflects and participates in the unity of all-encompassing Divine Love, and it is also love for the Absolute with all that we are. It is a whole and complete love, and every step along the way of Relief, every actualized virtue, is part of it. Thus, Charity is the fulfillment of Relief. With such a lofty definition, it is apparent that Charity is more of an aspiration than a final destination. It is a light constantly showing us the way to a more harmonious integration of Truth and Brotherly Love in all that we do, thereby making Relief a more present reality in the harmonious communion of our lives.

Masonry is obviously designed to provide its initiates with loving environments conducive to learning about and directly practicing the tenets and virtues with each other. Such work benefits us collectively and individually in many ways. For example, we can admire the same spark of inspired desire for goodness in each other while also sympathizing with our struggles to actualize that desire. While valuing our uniqueness and differences, we also see ourselves in others and others in ourselves, and thus embrace greater lucidity of oneness in the social dimension of our existence. Within the group, these observations amplify appreciation for the underlying commonality of our humanity, which facilitates experiences and expressions of compassion, which in turn catalyze greater interpersonal cohesion and harmony among us. At a more personal level, one may develop greater self-awareness (and thus lucidity) by witnessing in others various things, both positive and negative, that were previously unrecognized within oneself, things that were relegated to one's own Shadow. We can then grow in self-love through self-acceptance, self-forgiveness, and self-encouragement by internalizing the fraternal, gracious, and compassionate acceptance of imperfection in humanity, as well as the persevering devotion to continue to improve in virtue. This growth fosters greater wholeness, harmony, and oneness in our personal being, in our relationships, and in our communities.

It should be clear that conceptual learning about the tenets and virtues is not enough to instill them in our lives. We must also deeply contemplate them and practice mindfulness of them daily, fully integrating them into the way we live every moment. Doing so in group dialogue and shared prayer can be very supportive and facilitate insights and commitments that might not otherwise happen. An excellent solitary practice for supporting group processes is reflective journaling, making notes about how our recent thoughts, feelings, and behaviors either have or have not aligned with our aspirations. This can be done in a very structured way like that employed by Brother Benjamin Franklin, or it can be an informal kind of musing.[7] Some amount of both approaches is probably wise. In any case, such work facilitates consideration of the deeper significance of our tenets and virtues. We can more clearly see in our own experience how they bring human lives together, individually and collectively breaking down the illusion of separation and cementing bonds of love that more clearly reflect the Mystic Tie of our spiritual unity. We then share such reflections with each other, thereby energizing and encouraging mystical realization both individually and collectively.

ATTUNING WITH THE MYSTIC TIE IN FRATERNAL LOVE

This practice follows the same basic steps as the All-Seeing Eye meditation described in the previous chapter. You can move directly into this meditation after beginning with mystical prayer, or you can proceed from mystical prayer to the previous meditation and then to this one. An ideal time might be after you awaken and before venturing out into your ordinary interactions with human society and the world. As before, this mantra and image can also be silently practiced at various other times during one's day to reawaken to the truths they express. The mantra is now *omnia in harmonia*, Latin for "all in harmony." While chanting this mantra, hold an image of a symbolic red heart within the Square and Compass in your chest, radiating an aura, or blazing star if you will, of golden light, stirring pleasant positive feelings of love.

---

7. For more on Franklin's process, see Ellis, R., ed. (2017). *The Virtues Workbook: A Journal for Practicing Virtue According to Benjamin Franklin*, independently published.

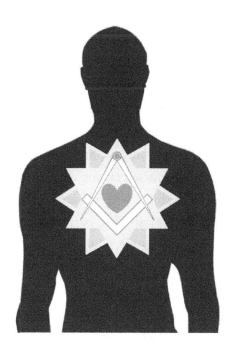

With each inhalation, feel the Divine Presence, the pure force of life itself, being breathed into your heart, making it turn a beautiful bright red. Experience the inhalation as having a refreshing cooling effect. With each exhalation, chant *omnia in harmonia*, visualizing the rays of the golden aura reaching out with love into all the world around you, and the color of your heart turning toward an equally beautiful purplish red. The sensual effect of exhalation is warm and soothing. Performing it in the middle of your vocal range and with your throat open and relaxed can help the vibrations resonate in your chest.

The Square and Compass represent the harmonious union of heaven and earth, of the Great Architect and creation, and, ideally speaking, not only within you but in our fraternal experience of the Mystic Tie. The changing visualization of the breath cycle is employed because the air we breathe is from the atmosphere that envelops all life on this planet. Its oxygen is the most immediately necessary element of our physical life and a common birthright shared among all human beings and countless other creatures. The carbon dioxide we exhale returns to the atmosphere to enliven the plants of this world, which in turn give back oxygen and many other things we need to survive and thrive. Thus, respiration is our constant participation in the cycles of the one life in which we all exist. What is true in the physical dimension is also true emotionally, mentally, and spiritually – as above so below, as within so without. Whatever good we cultivate within ourselves, such as loving thoughts and feelings about our connectedness with others, contributes to the unity, wholeness, and harmony of all. The performance of this meditation is simultaneously a very tangible, highly symbolic, and deeply spiritual participation in loving harmonious communion with the All and One, the Mystic Tie.

While we continue our personal practices, we should also consider that a more complete realization of fraternal love includes engaging with others of like mind. Thus, where possible, practices from this and the previous chapter can be engaged together by groups of Masons. A growing number of lodges, chapters, and other Masonic organizations welcome such practices within their tyled meetings, or within open or informal gatherings called specifically for such work. At the time of this book's writing, the author is unaware of any jurisdictions with regulations preventing the inclusion of contemplative activities, so long as they do not add to, interfere with, or supplant the authorized ritual forms. To the contrary, every form of ritual opening and closing *is* a contemplative practice when rightly understood. Furthermore, once a lodge has been duly opened, it is traditional that the Master may exercise personal discretion in providing and overseeing instruction. Such instruction can just as rightfully be delivered in the form of a guided meditation or group chant as in an historical lecture. Where the local environment is too oppressive to dare such efforts, Masons are certainly within their rights as ordinary human beings to gather privately for group practices related to their shared fraternal experiences as well as their individual contemplative pursuits. So, in one way or another, it is possible for sufficiently motivated Masons to experience the Mystic Tie in deeper and more harmonious communion with their fraternal companions. The following sections address how previous content can be adapted to that end.

HOLISM

In addition to routinely contemplating the physical, emotional, intellectual, and spiritual aspects of our individual being, we now also attend to each of them as part of our fraternal lives and relationships. For fraternal love to be as whole, harmonious, and revealing of oneness as possible, we must actively engage each of the four dimensions in our gatherings.

Physical wholeness is present in the interconnectedness of the different spaces, furnishings, and decorations of the lodge, temple, chapter room, and so forth, as well as in the physical interaction of the members with that place and with each other. Emotional oneness is in the interrelatedness of members' feelings and how their sentiments affect each other and tend to blend into a pervading atmosphere when they are together. This atmosphere can even charge the physical space of the room itself, so that walking into it, or even thinking about it, can change members' emotional states. In that effect, we begin to see a greater wholeness in how the emotional impacts the physical, and vice versa.

The reciprocal effects between the space and the psyches that gather there draw our attention to the intellectual aspect of our being. Group minds can form when everyone present focuses awareness on the same things, and especially when they are surrounded by and attending to the symbols they collectively revere and contemplate. This phenomenon does not necessarily mean that everyone is thinking the exact same thing with no room for deviation from prevailing opinions. When a group mind is healthy and functioning well, it is characterized by a synergy in which members share the experience of encountering new questions and achieving new insights together. Indeed, a crucial aspect of synergy is welcoming and respecting the divergent thoughts that can flow from the unique experiences, perspectives, and talents of each individual – they are also part of the whole. The harmonious integration of such diversity is what makes it possible for the group mind to be more than a closed system in which the same old ideas and attitudes simply recirculate as un-evolving norms that eventually choke the lifeforce out of the system.

Referencing the lifeforce of the Builder's Art brings us to its spiritual dimension, which is the essence of all being, and the source of the creative intuitions and inspirations that lead the group's synergy into those new places. Spirit is the aspect of the Craft that begets and unifies the others; it is the wholeness and oneness of the lodge manifesting in the interconnectedness and interdependence of its physical, emotional, and intellectual aspects. The factors of time and practice, including the integration of actions, feelings, and thoughts with the lifeforce of spirit, can further produce an *egregore* for the lodge. An egregore is not just a group mind, but a kind of living entity with its own unique character, which includes a drive to survive, perpetuate itself, and express its potential, just like other living beings. When the membership of a Masonic body intentionally nurtures the egregore with our tenets and virtues and the wholeness, harmony, and oneness of the Mystic Tie, then the egregore naturally develops to encourage and support the same for each member.

While we can easily connect the idea of spirit with the lifeforce uniquely manifesting within a group of Masons, it is also the most mysterious aspect of being. So, together we Masons honor the mystery of the Divine in many ways, not the least of which is through our quest for the Lost Word and its value to us as an emblem for the Ineffable. The sacred silence of our private meditations is also practiced within our lodge rooms when at labor, where the members are traditionally expected to remain quiet except when speaking as part of the ritual or for other official business. Of course, our moments of prayer and many words in our ritual certainly direct our thoughts and feelings toward the spiritual.

MYSTICAL PRAYER FOR THE LODGE AS A COMMUNITY

While prayer is already a part of all official Masonic labors, our traditional prayers are not often overtly mystical in nature, seldom obviously evoking both the spiritual union of the members as well as their individual and collective oneness with the Great Architect. Yet, each of us is free to interpret the usual lodge prayers according to our own best understanding. For instance, listen for hints of unity, wholeness, and harmony in this common prayer for the opening of a lodge.

> *Most holy and glorious Lord God, the Great Architect of the Universe, the giver of all good gifts and graces. Thou hast promised that, where two or three are gathered together in Thy name, thou wilt be in their midst and bless them. In Thy name we have assembled, and in Thy name we desire to proceed in all our doings. Grant that the sublime principles of Freemasonry may so subdue every discordant passion within us – so harmonize and enrich our hearts with Thine own Love and Goodness – that the Lodge at this time may humbly reflect that order and beauty which reign forever before Thy throne. Amen*

There are many possibilities to contemplate here, but for now we examine two. First is the phrase "in Thy name," which is commonly interpreted to mean something like "in Thy honor" or "under Thy authority." For mystics, however, a Divine name is not only a way of addressing Ultimate Reality in personal terms. To know the name of something or someone suggests some degree of familiarity, and so mystics often regard Divine names as having spiritual power to facilitate greater communion with some aspect of the One. When the Great Architect of the Universe is understood as the Ultimate Reality, the essence of the Mystic Tie, then the words "in Thy name" signify our intention to remember that we are presently communing *within* that mysterious No-Thing/Everything. This statement leads to the second phrase under consideration, which is "reflect that order and beauty which reign forever before Thy throne." Taken as a whole, these words clearly reference a state of perfect harmony, wholeness, and unity. Furthermore, this state is "forever before Thy throne," which is to say always and eternally present when reality is viewed from a transcendent perspective. With just these two examples, we can mystically interpret this traditional prayer as affirming that we are already in communion with God and renewing our desire to reflect that truth more intentionally and reverently.

A most noteworthy example of an overtly mystical prayer for a lodge community was penned by Brother Walter Leslie Wilmshurst (1867–1939). Wilmshurst was a self-avowed mystic and a highly praised author of numerous books and articles addressing the philosophy and spirituality of the Craft. He was also the founder of Living Stones Lodge #4957 in Yorkshire, England, where his teachings on mystical understandings and practice of Masonry are still applied. Regarding his prayer, the website of Living Stones Lodge says:

> *Wilmshurst encouraged every member of the Lodge at "high-twelve" every day to spend a few moments to 'banish every other concern from his thought and try to visualise, clearly and earnestly, himself and his fellow members gathered together in Lodge, in peace, concord and charity with each other' each reciting what has become known in the Lodge as "The Noon-Day Prayer."* [8]

8. See *Lodge of the Living Stones*, http://www.lodge-of-living-stones.org.uk/traditions.htm

Since its appearance, other lodges and individual Masons have adopted the prayer and Brother Leslie's recommended way of offering it. Here is the text of that prayer:

> *Here in the presence of the Great Architect and in fellowship with my brother Masons, I offer myself as a living stone of a building raised to the service of God and the Craft. May the power of the Highest overshadow and descend upon us! May light illumine and love unite us, that we may know ourselves one in God; and that from our unity there may go forth to all beings light, love, peace. Amen* [9]

Masons may also choose to create their own prayers for the invocation and practice of mystical fraternal communion. The same guidelines apply as those previously presented for personal mystical prayer, with the added condition of remembering and blessing our interconnectedness with our closest brethren. In any case, this kind of prayer is ideally practiced both individually and when a lodge or other group is meeting together. Whether through a traditional Masonic prayer, Brother Wilmshurst's prayer, or one originally composed for the purpose, the members of a Masonic body magnify the wholeness and harmony of their fraternal love by communing with each other in spirit, joining together on the way of oneness.

GROUP MINDFULNESS

While mindfulness often seems a principally individual practice, there is no reason that Masons cannot practice it together in groups. In fact, there are many benefits to doing so, certainly including a shared experience of the holism we have just been considering.

---

9. For more on this beautiful prayer and group spirituality, see Baker, T. (2010), "The Lodge of the Living Stones as a Group Mind," *Lodge of the Living Stones*, http://lodge-of-living-stones.org.uk/ARB%20Group%20Mind.pdf

The most important way for Masons to practice communal mindfulness is in our rituals. Every opening and closing, degree ritual, ceremonial reception of dignitaries, and officer installation, is an occasion to engage in group mindfulness.[10]

In mindfulness of ritual, individuals are not only being acutely aware of their own presence in the moment, but also know that others are doing likewise, sharing many of the same physical sensations, emotions, and thoughts, and being moved to do so by the same mysterious spirit. They recognize that together they are thinking, feeling, and acting as one, a beautiful organism enjoying its life, expressing itself according to its inherent nature and special purposes, and nurturing its constituent parts accordingly. No matter what their separate roles may be, every individual can align with others in this way, which certainly includes those observing. In fact, rather than merely being passive witnesses to ritual, observers can and should be active participants in helping to create and maintain the proper mental, emotional, and spiritual environment for Masonic labor. Such participation is vital to charging the room with a persistently harmonious and beneficial atmosphere.

REFLECTIVE DIALOGUE

At this stage of progress in the way of oneness, it is fitting for our personal practice to include reflection on the intersections of our internal lodges with the Masonic lodge, how the Divine within oneself interacts with Ultimate Reality manifesting in the tradition and society of Masonry. Bringing that practice into a group setting includes not only quiet time for our individual reflections, but the sharing and processing of those reflections together. Such dialogue

---

10. For more thorough treatment of contemplative group practice in Masonry, see Dunning, Jr., C.R. (2021). *The Contemplative Lodge: A Manual for Masons Doing Inner Work Together*, Stone Guild.

may or may not immediately follow a ritual, meditation, or other contemplative activity, but it is typically beneficial to provide at least a short period for everyone present to silently focus their minds on the matter to be discussed, then opening the floor for sharing. These reflections can touch on any or all the ideas and practices we have been considering and certainly the activities of the lodge or group itself.

One of the most valuable benefits of reflective dialogue is that it facilitates the development of truly supportive bonds between individual members, each of whom is bound to encounter very personal private challenges on their mystical quests. At various times before now, it has been noted that there are trials and risks in mystical practice. Furthermore, there can be significant differences in the details and nuances of the challenges and risks faced by one person versus another, complicated by countless internal and external factors. It is therefore impossible for any single book, even many volumes of books, to fully address any individual's (much less a group's) needs in mystical realization. Exacerbating all of this is the fact that none of us can see ourselves with perfect clarity or completeness, and we therefore need to see ourselves through the eyes of others to grasp more of the wholeness of self, certainly including its mysterious ineffable depths. Thus, we find much sagacity in the Craft's admonition that we should be willing to both give and receive assistance, counsel, and instruction. To recognize the benefits of seeking help, to humbly request it, and to accept it gratefully and graciously are self-loving examples of wisdom, strength, and beauty. To in turn be willing and able to offer support of this nature is certainly a meaningful expression of fraternal love. The following poem captures something of what such experiences can be like.

A PATTERN OF LIFE

Silken threads of consciousness

woven through our discourse,

a crystalline web

stretches between the branches

of two tall trees.

It sways there,

suspended as a bridge,

naturally designed,

constructed with intelligence

between the youngest green shoots

that have just begun

to open to the sun.

The dew beads upon its threads –

some to fall

and be sucked up by roots,

some to rise

and join with the clouds –

they are crystal balls,

each bending the refracted light

of the others

into a maze of colors;

dancing, dazzling jewels

strung in a pattern of life.

CHAPTER SIX
THE BLAZING STAR AND THE INTENDANTS OF THE BUILDING

The previous two chapters have moved through loving self into loving other Masons as vital to this mystical way of oneness. In this chapter, we focus on extending love even further through reflections on symbolism found in the Scottish Rite's 8th Degree, *Intendants of the Building*, especially as it is practiced in the Southern Jurisdiction of the USA. This degree has important messages about our nature as human beings and our relationship with Deity, and a call to action that is sorely needed in our times. In keeping with our obligations, we only reference things that are already found in publicly available versions of 8ᵗʰ Degree ritual. We also draw from authoritative commentaries on it, as well as look to the ancient wisdom tradition of Kabbalah as a catalyst for further insight. It must also be said that there are many other important lessons and symbolic elements of the 8ᵗʰ degree that are left for your own discovery and exploration.

The instructions of the current ritual state:

The Degrees of this Rite are not for those who are content with the mere ceremonies and uninterested in the mines of wisdom buried beneath the surface. How far you will advance in your understanding of Freemasonry depends upon you alone.

Here, as everywhere in the world, darkness struggles with light; clouds and shadows intervene between you and the truth.

When you become imbued with the morality of Masonry, and it is familiar to you, then be prepared to receive more lofty philosophical instruction.

In an older version of the ritual is added:

*Here, as in all the Degrees, you meet with the emblems and the names of Deity, the true knowledge of whose character and attributes it has ever been a chief object of Masonry to perpetuate. To appreciate His infinite greatness and goodness, to rely implicitly upon His Providence, to revere and venerate Him as the Supreme Architect, Creator, and Legislator of the universe, is the **first** of Masonic duties.*

Further, in a Scottish Rite textbook, *Morals & Dogma*, at the close of the chapter on this degree, is written:

> *The symbols and ceremonies of Masonry have more than one meaning. They rather conceal than disclose the Truth. They hint it only, at least; and their varied meanings are only to be discovered by reflection and study. Truth is not only symbolized by Light, but as the ray of light is separable into rays of different colors, so is truth separable into kinds.*
>
> *It is the province of Masonry to teach all truths--not moral truth alone, but political and philosophical, and even religious truth, so far as concerns the great and essential principles of each.*

Here we have a clear declaration that there are many ways to appropriately interpret the things we experience in Masonry, and in doing so, one of the primary aims is for us to know God more fully. So, let us consider how this degree is relevant to that aim. To do so, we reference Kabbalah, which is introduced in the 4th Degree of the current Southern Jurisdiction ritual, where it is explained as an indispensable aid for gaining deeper insight and understanding of the Rite.

Kabbalah is the esoteric tradition of Judaism, and one of its central symbolic systems is the Tree of Life, a diagram of ten basic divine powers or principles of creation, called *sephirot*, and illustrating their relationships with each other, as shown on the following page.

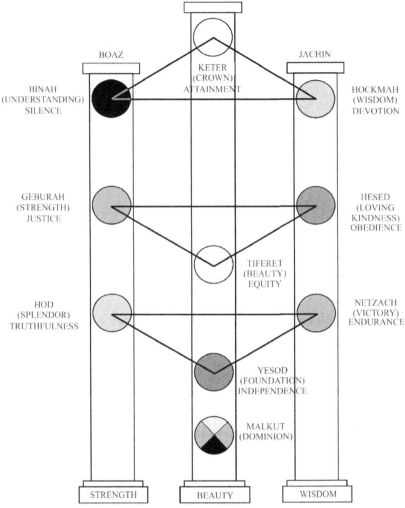

THE KABBALISTIC TREE OF LIFE
For each sphere is given the Hebrew name,
the English translation in parentheses, and
the virtue assigned in the 4th Degree of the A.A.S.R.-S.J.,
which does not assign a virtue to Malkut.
The columns bear the same Hebrew names in Kabbalah
and Masonry. At the base of the columns are the names
assigned to them as the Principal Supports of the Lodge.

In passing, we note that the Tree of Life also nicely overlays the Double Eagle of the Third-Third Degree of the Scottish Rite.

Much of the actual work in traditional Jewish Kabbalah is concerned with gaining deeper insight and understanding of scripture through various forms of contemplative practice. Kabbalists hold that it is possible to have more than one meaningful and valid interpretation of things and that these can be very different from each other without negating each other.

Let us start our work of seeking a deeper interpretation of symbols from the 8th Degree by going back to the beginning, the *very* beginning, as it is told in the book of Genesis.

> *In the beginning, God created the Heavens and the earth, and the earth was without form and void, and darkness was upon the face of the deep. And the spirit of God moved upon the face of the waters and God said, Let there be light, and there was light. (Genesis 1:1-3)*

In the Hebrew words of this scripture, the spirit of God is *Ruach Elohim*, and *ruach* is a Hebrew word that not only means "spirit" but also "breath." It is immediately after this spirit or breath moves that God gives birth to the light. Note the order here: breathing and then illumination. This order is followed later when God creates Adam by first forming his body from the soil, which is called *adamah* in Hebrew, and then breathing the breath of life, *Nishmat Chayyim*, into his nostrils. At that moment of receiving God's exhalation as his inspiration, Adam becomes a whole living being, not only alive but made in the image of God, illuminated with intelligence and with the ability to speak and thus capable of naming things.

On that note, let us give special attention to the Hebrew name of God used in these scriptures, which is *Elohim*. The *–im* suffix means it is a plural noun, and the actual Hebrew words of that text have God saying, "Let us make humans in *our* image." Here we have God, unequivocally insisted upon as the one and only Supreme Being by Jews, Christians, and Muslims alike, nonetheless referring to God's self in the plural. This is a mystery that ought to grab our attention, for it suggests that either our very scriptures contradict most of the theologies based upon them, or that there is a deeper understanding of both to be grasped.

With this mystery in mind, we can look to the 8th Degree and note that on one side of its jewel (to the right in the diagram on the following page) is the Divine name, *Achad*. As a noun, *achad* means "one," and our ritual tells us that, as a Divine name, it refers to the one God who is the Source of all. However, the word *achad* can also refer to a number of things that are united together as a whole. So, *Achad* as a name for God not only reminds us of God as the transcendent One who creates all things, but also the immanent One in and through which all things are united together. The name *Achad* is a reminder that nothing exists entirely separate from God, that God is

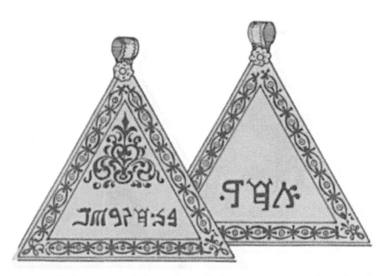

present in all things, and thus that all things are united in the dimension of spirit. *Achad* is a name for the One who is also many, like the name *Elohim* suggests a plurality that is still One.

Now let us turn our attention to the other side of the jewel (on the left), where we find the term *Ben-Khurim*. *Ben-Khurim* is traditionally translated from Hebrew as "Son of Nobles," where *ben* literally means "son" but may also mean a descendant or disciple, and *khur* means "noble." Khur is also directly related to the verb *khara*, meaning "to burn" or "to glow." Thus, the *khur* in Ben-Khurim conveys the more general sense of brightness and illumination. Once again, note that the *-im* suffix signifies the plural. To whom does this term actually refer? Who are these noble, bright, glowing ones, and who are their descendants or disciples?

These are questions not directly answered in the lessons of this degree. So, we should consider some different possibilities in response to this mysterious term. First, some Masonic scholars have speculated that the name Hiram is based on the word *khur*, so it is possible that Ben-Khurim is simply intended to mean one who is the follower of those who are like Hiram, a Mason.

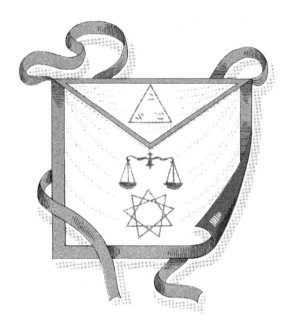

To get to another possibility, let us refer to one of the other key symbols of this degree. On the flap of the apron is a triangle bearing the initials (Hebrew in this diagram) for Achad, Ben-Khurim, and Shekinah. *Shekinah* is a feminine Hebrew word literally meaning a dwelling place, and it is used as a name for the presence of God in this world. According to many Kabbalists, Shekinah can be understood as the feminine personification of the Spirit of God mentioned at the beginning of Genesis, as well as the Holy Spirit, and Divine Wisdom (*Chockmah* in Hebrew, *Sophia* in Greek).

Divine Wisdom is clearly addressed as "her" in the book of Proverbs. Here is how she speaks of herself in Chapter 8 of that book:

> *The Lord possessed me in the beginning of his way, before his works of old. I was set up from everlasting, from the beginning, or ever the earth was. [...] When he prepared the heavens, I was there: when he set a compass upon the face of the depth. (Proverbs 8:22-23, 27)*

Shekinah is also the Pillar of Smoke and Flame that led the Israelites through the wilderness, and appeared in the tabernacle, and later in the temple, above the Mercy Seat on the Ark of the Covenant. She is therefore called the *Shekinah Glory* and the *Glory of God*. Keeping in mind that Masons dedicate our labors to the Glory of God, it should be no surprise that Shekinah has long been of interest to us. In Mackey's *Encyclopedia of Freemasonry* (1878), the entry on Shekinah reads:

> *The Shekinah was the symbol of the Divine glory; but the true glory of divinity is Truth, and Divine Truth is therefore the Shekinah of Freemasonry.*

> *This is symbolized by light, which is no longer used by us as a "substitute" for the Shekinah, or the Divine glory, but as its symbol -- the physical expression of its essence.*

Note that Mackey has just said that the light we seek in Masonry represents Shekinah, the Divine Glory and Truth of God. Many years prior to Mackey's statement, Shekinah was already associated with the Blazing Star of the Craft Lodge, as noted in the publication of John Browne's *Master Key through the Three Degrees* in the late 1790s. Then, in 1846, the Reverend Brother George Oliver also makes this connection in *An Apology for the Freemasons*, where he reviews the story of Genesis and says:

> *...the Shekinah, or blazing star from heaven, was placed as a guard to protect the tree of life. From this Shekinah proceeded that celebrated cabalistical symbol of the Deity called the Sephiroth, consisting of ten splendours, three of which are placed as the united light of God, or crown of glory.*

In the same paragraph, after citing the Kabbalistic text, *Sefer Yetsirah*, Oliver goes on to report this:

> *In one of the ineffable degrees of Masonry, called "Master in Israel," the blazing star is made to consist of five points, like a royal crown, in the centre of which appears the initial of the* **sacred name**.

We should note that "Master in Israel" is another name for the Intendant of the Building degree, and the *Franken Manuscript* of 1783 confirms Oliver's description of these symbols.

Then, in 1850, Oliver published a book entitled *Symbol of Glory; Showing the Object and End of Freemasonry*, in which he quoted the lecture from a version of the 4th Degree, Secret Master, which said, "I have seen a Blazing Star, or the Shekinah...." Several paragraphs later, in his own words he says, "The primitive Blazing Star of Masonry had five points." Further on in that chapter he offers this:

> *The continental definition is, [...] "the Blazing Star [...] represents the Sacred Name of God, as an universal spirit who enlivens our hearts, purifies our reason, increases our knowledge, and makes us better men."*

We should also note that, consistent with what Oliver reports, older versions of the 8th Degree apron bear a five-pointed star instead of the nine-pointed star in current use by the Southern Jurisdiction. Within that five-pointed star were three Hebrew *yuds*, each the initial of one of the three sacred names spoken along with the name Shekinah at an important moment in this degree. Furthermore, the McClenachan script for the 8th Degree, a script formerly used in the Northern Masonic Jurisdiction, specifies that over the Master should hang a Blazing Star, with five points, and in its center three *yuds*, all surrounded by an interlaced triple triangle. In the lecture of that version the Master also says:

> *You will still advance towards the light, towards that star – toward the star blazing in the distance - which is an emblem of the Divine Truth, given by God to the first men, and preserved amid all the vicissitudes of ages in the traditions and teachings of Masonry.*

Although we now use only the nine-pointed star in connection with the triple triangle of lights in this degree, the language of the ritual still refers to it as the Blazing Star and an emblem of Divine Truth, and still has the Divine name within it. Thus, we have the Blazing Star present in the 8th Degree in a way that clearly alludes to it as an emblem of Shekinah.

Among Kabbalists, Shekinah is not only revered as the Pillar of Smoke and Flame, Divine Wisdom, and the Holy Spirit; she may also be known as the breath of life, *Nishmat Chayyim*, that God breathed into Adam. This is a very important connection, because the story of Genesis tells us that we are all descendants of Adam, and the breath of life is inherited by all human beings. Therefore, among her other manifestations, Shekinah may be regarded as the breath and light of life within each of us, regardless of race, religion, politics, or any other factor that distinguishes one human being from another, even our sins. She is thus not only our spiritual connection with God but also with each other. We are all joined by the one divine spirit of life in and around all of us, even if we are not aware of it. Shekinah is thus one and the same as the Mystic Tie!

The book of Genesis makes it clear that Adam failed to understand and realize his oneness with God. Adam's ignorance of Shekinah as the light of truth and the breath of life within him meant that he could not fully appreciate the blessing of Eden, and so he and all his descendants were fated to suffer in our sense of separation from

God. Kabbalah helps us understand this more deeply by suggesting that Adam is often best understood as the whole of humanity rather than taken literally as an historical person. In this sense, Adam represents the totality of all who ever lived or ever will live. Yet, in either case, an esoteric reading of Genesis suggests that Shekinah nonetheless dwells in each of us, whether we know it or not. We would not be alive without our earthly matter, *adamah*, being wedded with her. But most of the time most of us are like Adam in that we do not realize her presence within, and we are therefore relatively unresponsive to her, which is to say that we who are supposed to be wedded to her are figuratively dead to her. She is thus the Great Widow, ever seeking to raise us to awareness of our birthright, our union with God, and our union with each other through her.

We may now understand the term *Ben-Khurim* more deeply and mystically. The bright glow alluded to by the root word *khur* is a reminder of Shekinah, the Blazing Star, the Glory of God, the essence of all nobility. The plurality indicated by the suffix *–im* gives *khurim* the meaning of all beings illuminated by her. For Masons to acknowledge one another as Ben-Khurim is therefore not unlike the traditional Hindu greeting, *namaste*, which means "I bow to the Divine in you." It is an acknowledgment that you and I, all of us, are of the Achad, the One who is the Source of All, the giver of the breath of life and the light of truth, present in this world and within us as Shekinah, the Mystic Tie.

Should anyone think that the present author, Mackey, Oliver, and others are merely asserting our own personal views in this interpretation, it should be noted that the shared identity of Shekinah, Divine Wisdom, and the presence of God within every soul is addressed in the 32nd Degree as the Holy Doctrine of Scottish Rite Freemasonry. There are numerous references to this doctrine in the *Scottish Rite Ritual Monitor and Guide*.

Having jumped from the 8ᵗʰ Degree to the 32ⁿᵈ, it is now pertinent to return to the 4ᵗʰ Degree, where the Master tells the candidate:

> *Like the light you bear, which yet you cannot see, Truth and the Lost Word, which are Light, are within reach of every man that lives, would he but open his eyes and see. The broad highway of Duty, straight as an arrow, leads directly to them....*

In that statement about "the light you bear," we may now recognize another allusion within the 4ᵗʰ Degree to the very same mystery we are examining in this degree. The lesson of that degree emphasizes duty as the means to awaken more fully to the light we already bear, the Blazing Star that we now know by the name *Shekinah*. The etymology of the word *duty* traces back to the Latin *debere* and *debitum*, which mean "debt." In short, a duty is a moral obligation to do something in return for something we have received. Furthermore, because duty as we speak of it here is a *moral* obligation, it cannot be something imposed upon us like a tax or some form of servitude. It must instead freely well up from the depths of the heart. So, if we feel a sense of obligation in gratitude for the Divine Breath of Shekinah, how are we to perform a fitting duty that puts our knowledge to practical use?

To begin making our way toward an answer, recall that when God created Adam, the stated purpose was not only to have him rule over all the earth and its creatures. More especially, humanity was meant to *tend and care* for the Garden of Eden in which God had placed the Tree of Life. In Kabbalah, Eden is often regarded as a metaphor for living in blissful awareness of the presence of God, not a place but a state of consciousness in which one is in constant communion with the Divine. It is in that state of consciousness that Adam was made to dwell. But Adam's initial innocence is the innocence of all human beings when we are infants; it is a blissful ignorance.

The story of Adam and Eve and their loss of Edenic innocence represents the natural developmental process for human beings. When we are first born, our consciousness is pure, simple, innocent, but also ignorant and foolish. Yet, even in infancy, like Adam, we start becoming aware of the complexity of existence, beginning with our own desires, our differences from each other, our vulnerabilities, and the suffering we cannot escape because of them. This awareness continues to grow, especially in the turbulence and anxiety of puberty and adolescence, so that by the time we are mature adults most of us consider ourselves completely separate individuals, and we feel some degree of aloneness in what seems to be an excruciatingly complicated dog-eat-dog world.

The legend of Adam's sons, Cain and Abel, portrays the terrible depths to which this suffering can lead. Cain's competitiveness, envy, and jealousy lead him to murder his own brother. When God asks Cain where Abel is, Cain replies, "Am I my brother's keeper?" Thus, Cain represents all of us who have forgotten that we are spiritually one with everyone else, whether we like them or not. Cain's actions, like those of the ruffians who slew Hiram, show us the worst consequences of that ignorance. The price Cain must pay is to travel even further from Eden, even deeper into the complex illusions of separation from God and division from other human beings.

The tales of Genesis can make it seem as if there is no way back to the peace and harmony of the Garden of Eden and the Tree of Life. Some people have even used them to teach that earthly existence is a prison we must endure until we leave this body after death. But we should recall that the underlying reason we suffer in this way is because we forget who and what each of us is – a Ben-Khurim.

Our duty, in gratitude for the life and light we have received, is therefore to think and act in ways that reflect our spiritual unity, our Mystic Tie, and thereby increasingly allow the Blazing Star of Shekinah, Divine Wisdom, to shine through us and dispel the darkness that is the illusion of separation from God and our fellow creatures. As a common opening charge for our Craft lodges says, "Wisdom dwells with contemplation. There we must seek her."

In our contemplation of this degree, or any other for that matter, we should carefully consider the title we each receive. In this case, it is *Intendant of the Building*. So, what is that building and how are we to tend it? A Kabbalistic interpretation of Genesis holds that all of creation was, and still is, sanctified by God. Recall that God clearly declares that each act of creation, and thus everything in the natural world, is good. We have not spoiled that basic fact. Our fall from Eden did not break creation. From a mystical perspective, the whole cosmos is still one great temple erected and inhabited by the Great Architect of the Universe. In terms of both an edifice and an ongoing construction project, it is the grandest building that we Intendants of the Building are charged to tend.

So, if creation itself is the building, then, in light of all we have seen, what does it mean to tend it? To answer that question, we contemplate words from the lectures in the McClenachan and *Magnum Opus* versions of the ritual and commentaries in *Morals & Dogma*, some of which are also referenced in the current Southern Jurisdiction text, *A Bridge to Light*. As you read, you are invited to breathe peacefully with an open heart and mind.

Masonry does not occupy itself with crying down this world, [...] nor exhort us to detach our hearts from this earthly life, as empty, fleeting, and unworthy, and fix them upon Heaven, as the only sphere deserving the love of the loving or the meditation of the wise. It teaches that man has high duties to perform, and a high destiny to fulfill, on this earth.... [...] It is here his influences are to operate. It is his house, and not a tent; his home, and not merely a school. He is sent into this world, not to be constantly hankering after, dreaming of, preparing for another; but to do his duty and fulfill his destiny on this earth; to do all that lies in his power to improve it, to render it a scene of elevated happiness to himself, to those around him, to those who are to come after him. His life here is part of his immortality; and this world, also, is among the stars.

[...]

The law of our being is Love of Life, and its interests and adornments.... Not a low or sensual love; not love of wealth, of fame, of ease, of power, of splendor. Not low worldliness; but the love of Earth as the garden on which the Creator has lavished such miracles of beauty....

[...]

Those only who feel a deep interest in, and affection for, this world, will work resolutely for its amelioration. Those who under-value this life, naturally become querulous and discontented, and lose their interest in the welfare of their fellows. To serve them, and so to do our duty as Masons, we must feel that the object is worth the exertion; and be content with this world in which God has placed us, until He permits us to remove to a better one. He is here with us, and does not deem this an unworthy world.

[...]

The brightness of the soul shines through this visible and sometimes darkened life; through all its surrounding cares and labors. The humblest life may feel its connection with its Infinite Source.

[...]

Thus earth, which binds many in chains, is to the Mason both the starting place and the goal of immortality. Many it buries in the rubbish of dull cares and wearying vanities; but to the Mason it is the lofty mount of meditation, where Heaven, and Infinity and Eternity are spread before him and around him.

[...]

There will always be in this world wrongs to forgive, suffering to alleviate, sorrow asking for sympathy, necessities and destitution to relieve, and ample occasion for the exercise of active charity and beneficence. And he who sits unconcerned amidst it all, perhaps enjoying his own comforts and luxuries the more, by contrasting them with the hungry and ragged destitution and shivering misery of his fellows, is not contented, but selfish and unfeeling.

[...]

He is the faithless steward, that embezzles what God has given him in trust for the impoverished and suffering among his brethren. The true Mason must be and must have a right to be content with himself; and he can be so only when he lives not for himself alone, but for others also, who need his assistance and have a claim upon his sympathy.

"Charity is the great channel," it has been well said, "through which God passes all His mercy upon mankind. [...] God himself is love; and every degree of charity that dwells in us is the participation of the Divine nature."

COMMUNING WITH THE MYSTIC TIE IN THE TEMPLE OF CREATION

To more fully realize the truth that we are always and everywhere within a grand edifice erected and inhabited by the Divine, and therefore in immediate contact with the material and social aspects of the Mystic Tie as well as the metaphysical, we can employ a method of visualization and chanting as we did in Chapters 4 and 5. This exercise can be done at any time, but is perhaps most appropriate at noon when the sun is at its zenith, or in the midst of one's usual daily activities and therefore most involved with the material and social world.

After achieving a sufficient degree of relaxation and mental centering, continue as follows:

1. Visualize yourself wearing a plain white Master Mason's apron. You might find it meaningful to first imagine yourself putting on the apron. As you stand there, try to feel the apron's presence on your body. If you prefer to have your body physically sitting for the meditation, then imagine yourself sitting on a large ashlar.

2. Once the experience of the apron is suitably clear and vivid, imagine yourself located on a checkered pavement with the column of Boaz to your right and Jachin to your left. These columns may be visualized in many ways, but there is great symbolic significance in Boaz being black and Jachin white.

3. Visualize the All-Seeing Eye in your brow and perform several repetitions of the chant as specified in Chapter 4.

4. Proceed to visualize the Square and Compass around your heart and perform several repetitions of the chant as specified in Chapter 5.

5. Focus on the Master Mason's apron on your lower abdomen and begin to chant the mantra *semper in templum*, meaning "always in the temple." Performing the intonation in a lower pitch may help with feeling it in your lower abdomen. As you inhale, try to feel the vital energy of nature itself being drawn to the apron, and as you exhale with the chant, see the apron glowing with a bright blue aura and feeling peaceful, harmonious, and joyful connectedness

with all things in creation. Planet Earth is often spoken of as the Blue Planet, and as the color of the atmosphere and its reflection in water, blue reminds us of the environment we have in common with all creatures in this world. Blue also naturally connects with the tradition of referring to a lodge of Master Masons as the Blue Lodge.

6. After several repetitions, cease the chant and refocus on the total image of yourself, clothed as a Master Mason, on the checkered pavement, with the Square and Compass around your heart, and the All-Seeing Eye in your brow. You may find that your awareness shifts from one detail to another, but with practice you can also develop the ability to experience more of it as an integrated whole in the same moment.

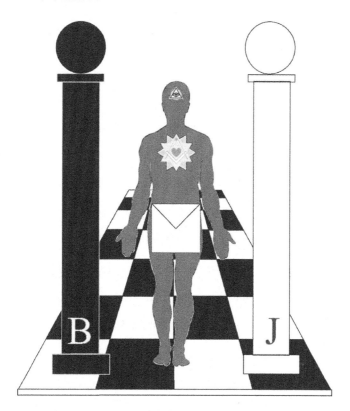

CONCLUSION

To begin serving as an Intendant of the Building is to be mindful that we, each and all, are Ben-Khurim, the children of bright shining Shekinah, the Divine Light and Holy Breath of Achad, the source and the unity of everything that is, or the Mystic Tie. Then, we may better fulfill our duty as Intendants of the Building in contemplation and mindfulness of our oneness with God, each other, and all that is, listening deeply for the voice of Divine Wisdom, the Glorious Holy Presence. The Blazing Star of Shekinah thus becomes our guide in continually serving Charity – selfless, universal, Divine Love – as our consistent aim in joyfully living with each other and tending to God's creation, this magnificent ongoing project that is the Temple of all Temples.

To close, here is a poem from contemplation of these themes.

THE BLAZING STAR OF MASONRY

O contemplate the Blazing Star

And let it guide your thoughts afar

From common notions about light

As it is sensed through earthly sight.

So, may the mystic quest begin

To fully know the Light within.

It shines unto your inner eye

More constant than the sun on high,

The power from which mind is wrought,

Projecting emblems of each thought,

It paints the scenes of fancy's flight,

And glows within your dreams at night.

Still, farther in beyond these veils,

It radiates through higher scales,

Where no figure, tint, hue, or shade

Fades or filters its pure cascade.

This beam that lights you like a lamp,

And seals your soul with Heaven's stamp,

Evoked with Holy Wisdom's breath,

And flowing from eternal depth,

This Glory on your Mercy Seat

That makes you whole, alive, complete,

Is the Presence of Truth Most High,

The essence of the Mystic Tie,

The shared flame of all creation,

The one root of emanation,

The light and life in everyone,

The ever-present inner sun.

And so, your life stands not apart,

But communes with all, heart to heart.

Thus, in love you most truly are

Illumined by our Blazing Star.

CHAPTER SEVEN
PATTERNS IN CONTEMPLATIVE LIFE

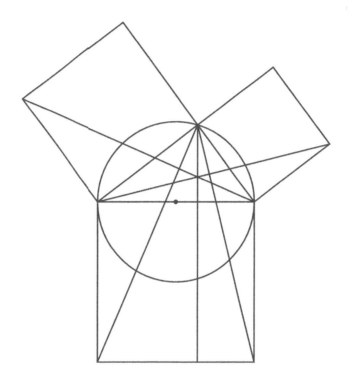

Contemplative practice is vital to mystical realization, yet the contemplative way of oneness within oneself, with the Absolute, and with all can sometimes be very demanding and difficult to navigate. Even so, these demands and difficulties are never entirely unique, and people who have been practitioners for many years have had the opportunity to observe certain recurring patterns in philosophical and spiritual callings that involve genuine inner work. By *inner work* we mean making use of methods that shift consciousness back upon itself, out of the usual states and functions, to open to and develop new possibilities of wisdom, strength, and beauty. In this chapter we reflect on some of these patterns and note their connections with various Masonic themes. Among the benefits of doing so is recognizing that one is not alone in facing the challenges of inner work and considering responses to those challenges that have been found useful by others.

GAMES MYSTICS PLAY [11]

At the core of mysticism is the inner work of (1) penetrating deeply into the mysteries of our existence, (2) making changes in consciousness to directly engage the energies and principles of those mysteries within ourselves, and thereby (3) facilitating mystical realization and the transformation of our being. Around that core are many things that beckon for our attention, time, and energy. All those things – whether objects, ideas, or activities – have some potential to facilitate experiences at the core of mysticism, but they can also become parts of distractive and diverting patterns. One way to understand such patterns is in the language of games. If you are like most human beings, you will see at least some glimpses of yourself in this list. You may also see ways these games intersect and reinforce each other.

DRESS-UP

The regalia, rituals, roles, and titles of mystical systems and traditions can all be profoundly meaningful and useful. However, they can also become the focus of a game in which the spiritual glamor in the pretense of performing great and important things becomes a substitute for doing them in real life. During such games, a group or individual might even go through the motions of practical inner

---

11. This section is an adaptation of Dunning, Jr., C.R. (2020), "Games Esotericists Play," *The Midnight Freemasons*, http://www.midnightfreemasons.org/2020/06/games-esotericists-play.html

work, such as an invocation or guided meditation, but there is little to no real shift in consciousness, or there is a lack of follow through with inner work outside the event itself.

TEA PARTY

Many of us find great joy in social gatherings with mystical atmospheres and themes. We can gather with kindred spirits, tell stories, sing, poke fun, laugh, share our latest quandaries and discoveries, and enjoy the good feelings and other benefits of relaxation, belonging, and togetherness. Even so, like Dress-Up, this kind of activity becomes more a game than a real benefit when it serves as a substitute for, or even a barrier to, our inner work rather than a source of motivation, encouragement, and support for doing it.

CONNECT THE DOTS

Every mystic knows it can sometimes be helpful to study different systems, schools, traditions, authorities, and other sources of information. Our comparisons and contrasts often reveal possibilities of awareness, understanding, and manifestation we might have otherwise missed, give us a greater appreciation of the bigger picture of things, and can produce temporary feelings of accomplishment and satisfaction. Yet this practice turns into a game as we addictively pursue those feelings, sacrificing more and more time to historical, intellectual, and symbolic minutia that might have been spent in more productive inner work. It can also become a game of trivia when we begin relishing the acquisition of names, dates, events, and other bits of information that we can recall and toss out at a moment's notice.

TREASURE HUNT

The process of initiation, mystical realization, and transformation is very much a process of discovery, and frequently of things that are not easy to come by. A poor reflection of that process is the game of eagerly searching for that next obscure, rare, or highly guarded bit of information, ceremonial experience, meditation, or breathing technique. This is often done with hopes that the next discovery will somehow magically facilitate a significant leap in lucidity, unity, wholeness, or harmony. The game of Treasure Hunt becomes most apparent when one realizes that chasing after such things takes precedence over consistently making use of readily available time for inner work.

House of Cards

Keeping and displaying physical tokens and instruments of mysticism can provide inspiring reminders of one's commitments and aids to actual practice. On the other hand, the accumulation of ceremonial paraphernalia, jewelry, relics, mementos, documents, books, artwork, and so forth, can become the House of Cards game. Like Dress-Up, it does so when these things are primarily used to support one's self-image as a mystic. It is also shown to be a distracting game when the actual practice of inner work cannot be done in their absence.

Hide and Seek

Many mystical traditions and teachers speak of the importance of practicing silence, discretion, and humility with regard to one's inner work and other mystic activities. Circumspection in mystical practice is also wise due to how misleading dualistic language is about That which transcends duality. The game of Hide and Seek manifests when we adopt attitudes and behaviors of circumspection, reserve, and aloofness merely to give the *appearance* of knowing and participating in profound mystical things.

Why do we play such games? One possibility is in simply failing to recognize that the core of mysticism is the inner work of initiation and transformation in the realization of unity, wholeness, and harmony. The portrayal of mysticism in popular media can easily give the impression that these games *are* mysticism. Even self-proclaimed mystics may unknowingly assume this field is only a more exotic and intriguing form of entertainment or social engagement, and that terms like *inner work, initiation, transformation,* and *realization* are just intriguing ways of talking about a peculiar category of concepts and social status.

There are deeper and more complex reasons for these games, and they are rooted in the fact that the prospect of mystical realization is inherently threatening to the self-image and ego. Hand in hand with the bright elevating symbolism of awakening, rebirth, peace, and joy, the dark specters of great tests, trials, and death are universally present in mystical lore. Beneath our superficial thoughts of mysticism lurk powerful questions about who or what we really are, who or what we might become, and how realization and transformation might shake up our lives and relationships. So, while our egos may be very attracted to the spiritual glamor of grandiose visions and the pomp and circumstance of mystical groups, or fascinated by the prospect of being the possessors or revealers of secrets, there are also deep fears, often hidden from our conscious awareness, of the unknown challenges, demands, and sacrifices we may face.

Understandably, we may not feel up to the task, but our moth-like souls are still drawn to the mystic light. We might therefore use these games to acquire what seem like the next best things, which are the trappings, language, and imagery of mysticism, or the *facades* of initiation, realization, and transformation. Even when we recognize the essentialness of inner work, we may use these pastimes to distract and divert ourselves from it, semi-consciously creating the excuse of being too busy with all the other activities. Furthermore, we can find opportunities to build up our egos through the games of mysticism, taking pride in the exercise of our intellects and comfort in the development of belonging and prestige within mystical social groups. These positive strokes may reinforce our avoidance of the inner work, and to some degree we may even convince ourselves that we really are undergoing transformation, when in fact there is more make-believe happening than anything else.

Finally, it is important to say that catching oneself in these games is no justification for shame, guilt, or self-flagellation; those things can also become distracting games. We are all human and we are programmed, even hardwired, to protect and preserve our egos. Additionally, all of us carry insecurities, existential anxiety, and emotional vulnerability, even when we are from the most loving and stable backgrounds. Whatever our reasons might be, including simply being content with the fellowship, fun, and fascination of mystically flavored socializing, there is no Masonic condemnation for choosing to not engage the inner work. It can be challenging enough to be honest with ourselves about what we really believe, what we really want, and what we really are or are not willing to do to get it. Even so, Masonry continually reminds us that it is a Craft, the Builder's Art, something that demands real labor of a specialized sort, rather than these game-like patterns.

REMEMBERING THE TRESTLEBOARD

An interesting thing about many of these patterns is that when individuals start encountering them, they often do not seem like patterns at all, but are instead very new and personal experiences. Whether the experiences are pleasant or unpleasant, it can appear as though they are unique to oneself, and so they can contribute to feelings of isolation, aloneness, and even a kind of alienation from others. Such feelings, perhaps especially the pleasant ones, can fuel an egoic sense of specialness, grandiosity, and even a kind of mania. On the other hand, the unpleasant ones may contribute to loss of self-esteem and self-efficacy, to harsh self-judgment, and even to anxiety and depression. All these symptoms can interfere with greater realization of wholeness, harmony, and unity.

Part of the problem here is cultural. Those of us living in industrial and post-industrial societies (now most of the world) are, to some extent, working against our cultural norms when we dive into contemplative pursuits. It is not that contemplative practices and experiences are foreign to our cultures, but that they have been largely relegated to a kind of specialization that diverges from the typical expectations and demands of our ordinary lifestyles and values. In other words, if you want to sincerely engage in a contemplative life with routine practices of being still and quiet, turning inward, shifting how your consciousness works and what it is focused on, then you are, simply and bluntly put, being weird and attempting to take time and space away from the usual flow of things. That is a fact, not a judgment, and it naturally brings with it certain challenges. Accepting that weirdness and getting comfortable with it are certainly among them.

In addition to the previously noted feelings and effects, one pattern within the larger pattern of our weirdness is to feel frustration, resentment, anger, even loathing and hostility toward our culture and the people around us who remain more aligned with it than we wish to be. Many contemplatives have struggled with powerful negative attitudes toward their employers, family members, and friends because these people were directly experienced as agents of resistance to their contemplative and mystical aspirations. It is also very common to feel guilt and shame about having those attitudes, especially when they have led to pushing people away, lashing out, or being unkind in other ways. Just being aware of the temptation to do those things may be quite disturbing. So, if you have had such experiences, please know that you are not at all alone. You feel moved to do something unusual with your life, and it is simply natural to experience resistance.

Projection is another and deeper pattern within these larger patterns. It is an ego defense mechanism in which something we do not want to fully deal with in ourselves is instead treated as if it is external to us, in the world around us. In this case, rather than directly facing some of our own internal resistance to embracing a contemplative lifestyle, we distort our perceptions of other sources of resistance and even imagine it coming from places where there may in fact be none. In effect, we allow other people and circumstances to take the blame for our own hesitance and ambivalence, which permits us to feel better about ourselves, maybe even seeing ourselves as noble victims persecuted by a stupid, diseased, and evil world.

As Masons, observing this pattern in ourselves can remind us of the lessons of the 24-inch Gauge and Common Gavel. Our first job as Masonic contemplatives is to be unflinchingly, yet compassionately, honest with ourselves about our time management and the vices and superfluities within us that obscure the deeper potentials we feel called to discover and realize in this life. Only then can we begin to have the clarity to see more of the possibilities already present for actualizing our contemplative aspirations.

Note that this first step is an act of interior communication – parts of self welcoming, accepting, and coming to clearer understanding of other parts of self. We have previously dealt with this process under the heading of Shadow work. That kind of internal communication prepares for and supports the external communication that is crucial to more effectively and peacefully establishing a contemplative lifestyle within ordinary society.

An indispensable part of our response to resistance is communicating with significant others about our contemplative aspirations. It is not unusual for the people closest to us to feel that our desires to change are threatening to our relationships with them. They sense us becoming different, are aware of its effects on our attitudes and actions, and they begin to speculate on where things are headed. The less they understand what is happening, the more likely their reactions are to be shaped by suspicion, anxiety, and defensiveness. That is perfectly human!

In forthright communication with others, we are acting by the Plumb, the tool that urges us to be upright, authentic, and genuine. That means sharing with others why we want to pursue contemplative practice, how we think it can benefit us and those around us, and what we see as necessary conditions for the work to proceed. Very importantly, it means being fully honest and open about our own lack of complete understanding, acknowledging that there are plenty of mysteries about living a contemplative life, and that welcoming those mysteries, stepping into the unknown, is a necessary part of the quest.

We also need to be on the Square, talking about and demonstrating the Faith, Hope, and Charity that motivate us, and openly committing to the virtues that can continue to guide us as we trek through this new territory. These steps necessitate working *with* our dearest others, partnering with them in figuring out how we can continue to be good companions, even if we are walking the road of life in a way that is not yet as familiar.

In that last comment, we find allusions to the Level and the Trowel. The Level is an implement of the Craft that reminds us that we are all walking on the same plane of life in this world. No matter how different or alone we may feel, the fact is that we are not actually totally alone. Whether contemplative or not, everyone is facing the same fundamental existential demands. We are also all interconnected with each other, our attitudes and actions inevitably affecting each other to some extent. Rather than foolishly trying to deny or escape that interconnectedness, the Builder's Art supplies us with the Trowel, the Master Mason's tool of loving cooperation and collaboration. It makes possible the processes by which we create peaceful, harmonious, joyful, and productive coexistence, a unity with others who are very different from us in some ways.

The more fully we employ these lessons of the Craft's working tools, the more we are actively engaging a contemplative way of life. Thus, we become less fragmented and out of harmony with ourselves and with those people most important to us and to whom we are most important. It is all right there in the patterns on the Trestleboard.

LABOR AND REFRESHMENT

In the previous section, we addressed responding to perceived resistance to our practice from the world around us. One of the implicit factors in that reflection is the need to have a discipline in contemplative life, a commitment to a routine with a certain amount of frequency, duration, and consistency in one's contemplative sessions. In this section, we draw on Masonic ideas of labor and refreshment to address some issues with discipline and routine, including certain attitudes that may or may not be helpful.

Every serious teacher of contemplative practice asserts the value of such discipline, and every sincere practitioner has some sense of what seems ideal. Commonly, the expectation is at least one session every day, with some minimum amount of time spent doing a particular practice. Depending upon the system or tradition in which one practices, there may also be an understanding that with progress there should generally be an increase in frequency and duration of sessions toward an idealized goal.

So far so good. Contemplative practices such as meditation, mindfulness, and devotional rituals are like anything else that requires actual experience for the refinement of skills and understanding. If you want to be a good dancer, musician, painter, or archer, then you must work at it; labor is indispensable to more fully realizing and actualizing your potentials.

These analogies can be very helpful for several reasons. First, they illustrate that one is not likely to jump into any contemplative practice and immediately experience the states or effects known by journeyman practitioners, let alone seasoned elders. Second, they allude to the importance of focus in one's work. For example, it might be natural for someone to be simultaneously interested in a variety of things, but it would be nearly impossible to do justice to any one of them by flitting back and forth between them. Priorities must be established if noteworthy progress is to be made in any art, craft, or science. Third, the analogies suggest the invaluable benefits of working with the counsel of someone who already has a considerable amount of experience and understanding with the practices you wish to engage. Books and audiovisual media can be helpful, but due to the complexity of real-world application and individual differences, there is no substitute for spontaneous human interaction. Fourth, they help communicate that the work has ups and downs, periods of apparent progress contrasting with times that seem like plateaus or even regressions, and phases of enthusiasm and excitement versus others of apathy and boredom.

Noting all these parallels with more ordinary interests can sometimes be discouraging. Such a reaction can relate to the extent that desires for escapism or entertainment are among one's motivations for contemplative practice. Those motives are likely present for most people to some extent, and becoming more aware of them and others is always part of the work. These analogies can also be discouraging, because we perceive our lives to be already filled with demands on our time and energy. For busy people, committed contemplative practice can sound like just another thing to add to an overcrowded to-do list and might raise the difficult decision of rearranging schedules and perhaps even sacrificing something. Without any judgment at all, it is easy to see why many people simply choose to not pursue a contemplative discipline.

There is also a particular mental habit that can be a huge impediment to making a commitment to practice, which is all-or-nothing thinking. For one reason or another, people can get the idea, and communicate it to others (intentionally or not), that if you are not willing to go all in with maximum devotion and discipline, then you should not even bother. If one wishes to become a monastic or a hermit, then there is some reason for this belief, but that is not what Masonry calls us to do. We are to be workers in the ordinary world, and by working on ourselves in virtue and love we aim to become more beneficial to the wholeness and harmony of the world around us. It is worth noting again that the first tool we are given for that work is the 24-inch gauge, teaching us to manage our time wisely among three primary categories: (1) our usual vocations, (2) service to the Divine and others, and (3) rest and refreshment. Contemplative practice can be interwoven with all those categories in different ways, but the idea of constantly sitting in meditation or prayer, or performing studies or ritual, is obviously far from what the lesson of this tool intends. Of course, that extreme example is already irrelevant for most of us, yet we must each address the problem of balance in our lives and determine what a genuine commitment entails within our own contexts.

Just as the questions of frequency and duration of sessions call for a dose of realism, so does the matter of consistency over longer periods of time. Here again there is a kind of idealized aim for a truly committed practitioner to never miss a day, let alone a week, a month, or longer. Surely there are some individuals who have managed to structure their lives in ways that make it possible to rarely skip even one day, but many practitioners leading ordinary lives do indeed go through varying periods of less contemplative activity. Sometimes life throws unexpected obstacles in our way, and we must adjust on the fly, recognizing that for some length of time our own values urge us to prioritize something else over our preferred routine of contemplative practice. Other times, it may be that something internal is encouraging us to take a break, perhaps for reasons we do not fully understand, yet the urge is undeniable.

In any case, the idea of calling ourselves from contemplative labor to refreshment can be accompanied by unnecessary feelings of fear, shame, and guilt. Indeed, such feelings are sometimes intentionally stoked by people attempting to motivate themselves or others, but this tactic is not very productive in the long run. It would be more helpful if long-term practitioners were forthcoming about their own twists and turns with frequency, duration, and consistency. One benefit of such disclosures would be to show that all is not lost when one steps back for a while. Depending on the extent of the interruption, there might be some time needed to regain lost ground and begin again to make progress. On the other hand, a burst of exceptional progress can sometimes come on the heels of a hiatus. We are complex, multidimensional creatures, and sometimes there are dynamics occurring at deeper levels that we cannot grasp until after they have outwardly manifested, if even then.

To conclude this section, here are some suggestions on how anyone can start, or restart, a commitment to a contemplative routine. Try beginning with something small, such as a single 5-minute break at roughly the same time every day. Rather than a specific time on the clock, seek a convenient moment like just after getting out of bed, just before going to bed, or immediately before or after a meal. For those few minutes, do a simple contemplative activity that has immediately tangible rewards, like relaxation, breathwork, chanting, or silent prayer. If noise from the surrounding environment is an issue, consider using earplugs or noise cancelling headphones, meditative music, or something like white or pink noise. Another aid to consistent practice can be communicating with one or more people who also value contemplative routine, perhaps even meeting online for meditation together. Aside from these ideas, be creative about establishing contemplative practice as one of those things done on most days, like taking a shower. No matter what, just keep trying in whatever way seems to make sense, even if it is constantly shifting. Like caring for physical wellness and hygiene, one might miss some days of being intentional about it, but doing something more than nothing still has benefits. Finally, it is important to allow oneself to feel good about these efforts, even if they are judged as less than preferable. Those positive feelings are good for us; they engender inner harmony and wholeness and thus actually help us move toward greater fulfillment of our aspirations on the way of oneness.

A WAY OF BEING VERSUS A THING FOR DOING

Earlier, we recalled the 24-inch Gauge and its relevance to cycles of labor and refreshment in contemplative practice. There are limits to that analogy beyond which some confusion might arise. For example, it might be easy to associate contemplative practice with only one or two categories of activity associated with this tool, rather than understand and pursue its applicability to all three. This mistake may especially occur if one thinks of contemplative practice only as a special set of activities to do during particular moments or situations.

One pattern frequently observed among aspiring contemplatives is realization that the greatest fulfillment of their hopes for practice comes with expanding it beyond the times set aside for doing routine work, whether solitary or with a group. Whatever we seek – peace of mind, a richer or more joyous experience of life, healthier relationships, transcendence of self, deeper awareness and participation in love, or communion with the Divine – our quest is not something we can completely fragment from the other parts of our lives. Just like the 24-inch Gauge, our lives are a continuous and interconnected unity, not a loosely held collection of separate unrelated pieces.

Note that the title of this chapter is about contemplative *life*. We are talking about a *way of being*, not just something to do that is added to an otherwise ordinary lifestyle (although that might be how we initially get things rolling). By comparison, our ritual makes it abundantly clear that Masonry is about far more than what happens in the lodge or among members of the Fraternity. The tenets and virtues of Masonry are meant to be integrated into how we think, how we manage our emotions, passions, and desires, how we treat others, and how we relate to the Divine; they are directed to every segment of the 24-inch Gauge and thus to every part of one's 24-hour day. A Mason leading a contemplative life knows that every moment is an opportunity to actualize one or more of our Craft's ideals, including our oneness with the Mystic Tie.

To live this way is to both seek and radiate the light of wisdom in all that we do. According to a sadly too often neglected or forgotten charge at the opening of a lodge, "Wisdom dwells with contemplation, there we must seek her." Thus, to fulfill more of our potentials as Masons, contemplation should become more than something we do only in our private moments or in groups gathered to practice together. Furthermore, there is a dynamic relationship between (a) our times dedicated to meditation, study, or ritual and (b) how we interact with the world, the Divine, and our own selves in everything else we do. Our work in these two areas can and should support and refine each other.

So, let us reconsider three contemplative practices that can be flexibly employed across many situations in our lives – mindfulness, prayerfulness, and reflection.

Mindfulness is about being more fully present in whatever is happening at a given moment, not just externally through our senses, but also internally with awareness of the body, emotions, and thoughts. It involves openness to experiencing what is happening as fully and clearly as possible and a nonjudgmental acceptance of its reality. This is not to say that one never makes any judgments, but rather that we avoid making the kind of hasty or habitual judgments that distort our perceptions, lead to misunderstandings, and produce poorly considered actions.

Prayerfulness is about openness to the Divine, the Mystic Tie, and oneness in the present moment. It begins with humbly acknowledging that one's personal awareness of self and the world is limited in scope, power, and intelligence. Prayerfulness is about remembering that we are always surrounded and interpenetrated by mystery, yet also constantly connected with parts of the soul that transcend one's sense of self, and that we are ever in communion with the Great Mystery. Thus, prayerfulness keeps us open to the possibility of intuition, inspiration, and even revelation providing us with deeper awareness and understanding of any moment, its significance, and its potentials. It also helps us transcend narrow self-interestedness and be more fully awake to the interconnectedness of everything.

One way to help make mindfulness and prayerfulness more habitual is to establish cues for them, little happenings that remind us to be mindful and prayerful. The Buddhist teacher Thich Nhat Hanh used the example of the phone ringing as a cue to be mindful when answering and conversing with the person who called. We can train ourselves to respond to even the most common things as prompts for mindfulness and prayerfulness, such as hearing bird songs or the hum of an electric motor like those in refrigerators. There are countless possibilities, and it begins by frequently repeating an affirmation to oneself: "Whenever I become aware of _____, it serves as a reminder of mindfulness and prayerfulness." Eventually, the cue automatically does its desired job, and frequent repetition of the affirmation is no longer necessary, although it might help to come back to it from time to time.

Reflection is the process of taking time to carefully think back on an experience, recalling it as clearly as possible, and trying to gain even further insight into what happened, how we were affected by it, and what can be learned from it. Reflection provides us with the best opportunity to note the relationships between what happens in our dedicated times of meditation, study, or ritual and the other moments of our lives. We can then evaluate how well we are integrating the teachings of Masonry throughout the various parts of our lives and consider how we can use that information to improve in this "progressive art."

In essence, reflection is the practice of debriefing with ourselves, which can be done either quickly on the fly or more thoroughly in times specifically set aside for the purpose. With a little mindfulness, we can easily discern that there are many occasions in our daily lives when it is naturally fitting to pause for a moment to revisit something with questions like these:

- What just happened?

- How did it affect me and others physically, emotionally, mentally, and spiritually?

- How mindful and prayerful was I?

- To what extent did I respond in ways congruent with the principles, tenets, and virtues I most value?

- What could I learn and apply from this experience?

It can be very helpful to jot down notes about our reflections, even if we never look at them again. Just the act of writing something down helps us mentally anchor and clarify it.

Let us begin wrapping up this section by noting that becoming more mindful, prayerful, and reflective commonly leads to slowing down, both internally and externally. Many of us have been conditioned away from such healthy ways of being. Instead, we have become overcommitted and are frequently in a rush. We are not only trying to get the present thing done as quickly as possible, but also anticipating the next thing we might be doing, and perhaps having lingering thoughts and feelings about the last thing we did because we did not give ourselves time to reflect on it before moving into the current thing. Thus, we are not as fully awake to the present moment and its interconnectedness as we could be – we are just *doing*, not really *being*. That lifestyle is so pervasive in today's world that it can seem most acceptable, praiseworthy, and even comfortable in some respects. But it comes with great costs as we habitually and senselessly hurry past the things that most of us, in our heart of hearts, believe are the most important parts of life. So, let us end with these questions: What lifestyle best serves your deepest hopes, intentions, and aspirations, and most helps you avoid fragmentation and being at odds with yourself? What is your most Masonically inspired answer to that question? How can you move further into the way of life you feel most inwardly called to live?

MYSTERY AND APPRENTICESHIP

When making a sincere effort at contemplative practice, one cannot fail to make important observations about consciousness. In this section, we consider some common observations and various implications under the heading of "Mystery and Apprenticeship." These two terms are naturally related, because it is the mystery of a craft that makes apprenticeship within it beneficial. Smart apprentices know there is much that they do not know, including that they are not aware of all the ways they lack knowledge. Rather than responding to their ignorance with nothing but fear, indifference, or pretense, they humbly, yet eagerly and joyfully, commit to learning and growth. Furthermore, they understand that their best development comes not only from their own process of trial and error, but also with the instruction and counsel of others who are more learned, experienced, and skilled.

In the craft of contemplation, among the most common observations is that we cannot always make our minds do what we want them to do or stop doing what we do not want them to do. This issue is frequently noted by people as they begin working at focusing and quieting the mind. Despite its commonality, the problem is apparently shocking to some people and often discouraging. Many people claim such experience as evidence that they cannot practice mindfulness or meditation, taking the attitude that their minds simply do not work in the way they believe is necessary.

It is true that various peoples' minds can work somewhat differently. For example, some people find it hard to clearly visualize things. Aligning thoughts in a logical progression is challenging for others. Some find it difficult to name emotions, and others have a hard time with ignoring their physical sensations or with holding concentrated focus on one thing. It is almost always the case that such difficulties are symptomatic of underdeveloped abilities and that significant progress can be made with consistent efforts. Where there is indeed an intractable limitation, finding a different approach to contemplative practice is helpful. In these respects, contemplative practice is no different than becoming skilled at any art, craft, or game, and a more seasoned practitioner can help with the necessary learning and growth.

In seeing that we do not have as much mental control as we might like, another observation can arise, which is that we are mysteries to ourselves. Even in ordinary non-contemplative experience, we know there are things happening inside us that we are not aware of, let alone intentionally controlling. At the physical level this is obvious and easy to accept, and most of us are happy that we do not have to keep telling our hearts to pump, our guts to digest our food, and so on. It is not unsettling for most of us to acknowledge that our bodies are doing far more without our awareness and control than with them. However, for some people, it can be very troubling to realize that the same is true of the psyche. An iceberg is a popular analogy for this truth, but we will ponder a natural fountain in this context. Just consider for a moment all the invisible subterranean things that must be happening for a stream of water to gush up out of the earth. Even what we can see of a majestic geyser like Old Faithful is miniscule within such a context. In much the same way, there is an immense depth, breadth, and complexity of unseen biological, psychological, social, and spiritual factors giving rise to the fountain of a personal self, the relatively small natural wonder that each of us experiences as "me."

The mystery of self raises several implications, not least of which is the foolish hubris of believing we can fully understand or control any other person, or a group, community, nation, or human-ity, not to mention the Supreme Mystery of God. As some of our rites remind us, the great dictum posted in the forecourt of the ancient temple of Delphi was *Gnothi Seauton.* The special purpose of this temple was to house an entranced priestess who would speak prophe-cies in response to seekers' queries about mysteries encountered in their lives. Yet, before entering the temple, that brief maxim, "Know Thyself," served as a universally applicable preface for whatever might be spoken within the temple. This small and seemingly simple state-ment was regarded as so profound by legendary philosophers like Pythagoras and Socrates, that they insisted that it was the key to all wisdom. This is perfectly logical, because one's own consciousness with its unique perspective on the world is the instrument by which everything else is perceived, understood, and responded to. It then follows that the degree to which we have or have not become skillful with that instrument determines the degree to which we can reliably grasp and manage anything else. It is therefore entirely fitting that the tradition of Masonry continually urges us to attend to our own self-awareness and transformation, and, in doing so, refine the insight and virtue we bring with us into all our endeavors and relationships. In other words, this is part of the way that we make ourselves more fitting as living stones within the one whole temple of the Mystic Tie.

A significant challenge in this work is that this very instrument of one's personal consciousness must somehow learn to better grasp and manage itself and do so despite the fact of its self-ignorance. Imagine a cloudy mirror that could somehow fold to reflect on itself. In doing so it compounds its cloudiness! This imagery is an apt analogy for how contemplative practice can sometimes lead us to fall prey to our own misperceptions, fantasies, and delusions. Most conscientious contemplatives have occasionally winced or chuckled at themselves in hindsight, realizing that something they had believed was a deep clear insight proved to be nothing more than a reflection of their own hopes, fears, or biases.

The mystery of self and the implications and challenges that come with it brings us full circle back to the relevance of apprenticeship. For very good reasons, the Builder's Art teaches us that we should seek the instruction of more experienced workers and the counsel of the wise. The model of our mysteries illustrates that there is a natural developmental progression in our work toward wholeness, realization of oneness, and harmonization with all. That progression is optimized by learning from those who have gone before us, and what they have to offer is not only through example and instruction. They may also serve as mirrors in which we see ourselves from different perspectives. Just as an actual mirror shows us the physical face we cannot see with our own eyes, so can the mirror of a more seasoned contemplative reveal to us things we would not otherwise perceive in ourselves. Some of those things may be very pleasant and good, while others may not. So, the risks of apprenticeship include permitting the intimacy required for more of the naked truth of oneself to be seen by another. Given that it can be hard enough to accept the ugly truths of oneself, let alone allow them to be unveiled by others, it is not surprising that many people avoid apprenticeship in their contemplative lives. More is the pity because the most beautiful boons are gained by passing through such trials, which books and solitary experimentation cannot fully provide.

Apprenticeship is an immensely powerful opportunity to directly experience the transformative potential of Masonry's Principal Tenets – Brotherly Love, Relief, and Truth. This gift is like a rare and invaluable coin, on one side of which is a sign of the relieving truth that the same mystified and struggling humanity within oneself is also within those we most admire. On the other side is the emblem of Divine Light shining through the eyes of one of its children to lovingly witness and welcome itself shining through the eyes of another. In summary, contemplative apprenticeship is one of the most immediate and joyous ways we can more fully know and serve the wonderous reality of ourselves, harmonious unity with each other, and mystical oneness with the Divine. What greater purposes can there be for a contemplative life?

CONTEMPLATION, VIRTUE, AND LIGHT

Just as we previously noted that contemplative practice can lead us to appreciate our lack of complete self-awareness and self-control more fully, it can also lead us to more clearly perceive that the ordinary processes of cognition are not the only things happening in our psyches. These "ordinary processes" include intentionally attending to our sensations, recalling memories, generating words, numbers, and images, and putting different bits together in logical ways. Each of these are important activities that deserve attention and skill development. However, there are times when the light of a new insight or possibility pops into the midst of awareness, seemingly out of nowhere, obviously not produced simply through step-by-step mental construction. These events also deserve attention and understanding, especially among contemplatives, whose practices can lead to more frequently witnessing, evoking, and making good use of them.

Most people, contemplatives or not, know something about what these enigmatic happenings are like. In everyday language, we use certain words to speak of them, such as *intuition, inspiration, epiphany,* and *revelation*. We often describe these moments as if having a flash of insight, seeing a vision, hearing a voice, or getting a gut feeling, any of which can be very literal. In fact, occasionally we sense the very beginning of their emergence, and we may then pause to focus inwardly with the expectation that they unfold into something recognizable. While such phenomena are commonly known, they are the specialty of exceptional innovators in every field of human endeavor, including creative artists, inventive scientists, pioneering physicians and therapists, groundbreaking philosophers, and the true prophets of spirituality. They can also be signs of contemplative progress in the Builder's Art.

In the Masonic tradition, we celebrate these potentials through mythic references to things like Jacob's dream of the ladder between heaven and earth, and Hiram Abiff's prayers before drawing designs for the Craft's labors. Our traditional story of Pythagoras discovering the 47th Problem of Euclid says that he sacrificed a hecatomb immediately afterward. The claim that he offered such a sacrifice indicates that he regarded this discovery as of a divine nature, a gift of revelation and not merely a product of his own thought processes. There are further examples in some of the rites beyond the Craft Lodge.

In short, we are talking about a shift of consciousness that makes way for a different kind of knowing, a non-ordinary kind, maybe even a divine kind. We can also find such a shift alluded to by the ascension of the Winding Staircase *beyond* the Five Senses and Seven Liberal Arts and Sciences. That ascent certainly implies a kind of knowing in which we have passed beyond ordinary cognition, and in some jurisdictions is overtly said to transcend all that can be known by reason alone. Recall from Chapter 3 Plato's Divided Line and the ascent from the Visible Realm into the Intelligible Realm, and then through dianoia toward noesis. With that ascent in mind, consider this monitorial comment about the steps of the Winding Staircase:

> *They represent the progress of an inquiring mind with the toils and labors of intellectual cultivation and study, and the **preparatory** acquisition of all human science, as a **preliminary** step to the **attainment of divine truth**, which it must be remembered is always symbolized in Masonry by the WORD. (Daniel Sickels, General Ahiman Rezon, 1871, emphases added)*

It is no wonder that many Masons have regarded the letter G as referencing *gnosis,* or divine knowledge, as appropriately as it does God and Geometry, even if that connection is not explicitly made in our ritual. Indeed, there are two traditional practices at the opening of a lodge that reinforce this view. One is the opening charge that reminds us to seek Divine Wisdom in contemplation, and the other is invoking the aid of Deity at the beginning of our labors. Both practices suggest that we open our hearts and minds to divine guidance, something we cannot merely think up on our own.

Teachers and devoted practitioners in all the great contemplative and initiatic traditions have observed that there is a relationship between this divine way of knowing and the practice of virtue. The Craft is no exception, as highlighted by this reference from the Third Degree: "The All-Seeing Eye [...] pervades the inmost recesses of the human heart, and will reward us according to our merits." In this context, "merits" refers to virtues, which are not merely about following a behavioral code of dos and don'ts. As Aristotle clarified over 2,300 years ago, virtue is about internally discerning and externally enacting the middle way of balance between the extremes of excess and lack. Such discernment is improved through the mental disciplines of contemplation, such as mindfulness, meditation, reflection, and dialogue. In turn, one's ability to discipline and focus the mind is enhanced by the greater sense of wholeness, harmony, peace, and unity that generally results from the practice of virtuous behaviors and attitudes in the world; there is a reciprocal relationship. Intentionally pursuing both contemplation and virtue is therefore part of a very ancient pattern in which aspirants more freely experience and benefit from divine kinds of knowing, and they are thus empowered to have a more beneficial impact on the world.

While it is easy to describe the experience of non-ordinary knowing in very positive terms, it can also come with challenges. For example, it can be tempting to think that non-ordinary events are simply the outcome of one's own decisions and actions to enter different states of consciousness, as if the intentional shift is the cause of such a happening rather than a facilitative factor for it. In effect, the ego takes credit for creating something that it only desires, experiences, and recognizes. Intersecting with this pattern is another in which one has difficulty distinguishing between the emergence of divine knowing and perception of their own repressed or suppressed thoughts and feelings. Similarly, it can be easy to misinterpret a genuine epiphany as we filter it through the lenses of the psyche. In both cases, we find the folly of regarding one's own wish-fulfilling fantasies as spiritual revelations, or one's self-serving and biased impulses taken as divine commands.

These patterns of confusion are quite human and everyone following a contemplative path must encounter and work through their own relatively unique challenges with them. Note that their uniqueness for any individual is qualified as *relative*, for there is much about the entire process that is common and recognizable to those with greater experience. This benefit of greater experience is yet another reason to value the role of apprenticeship and openness to instruction and mentoring discussed in the previous section. We can also again see the great importance of the deliberative discerning element of virtue, the responsibility of contemplatives to examine their non-ordinary experiences carefully and critically in the process of exercising good judgment. A strong temptation to jump to conclusions and rush into action is frequently a red flag that one's own psyche may be distorting a deeper truth for less noble purposes. The true value of such events is often only clarified through further disciplined contemplation across longer periods of time, like days, weeks, and perhaps even years.

Finally, returning to the quote about the Winding Stairs from the *Ahiman Rezon*, we see that the Word of Masonry, also called the *Lost Word*, is one title for the kind of revelation we have been considering. We also recall that there are two traditional short answers to what we seek in Masonry, each expressing the same thing in a different symbolic way – one being the Lost Word and the other is Light. As we have seen, the highest attainment of this goal of knowing wholeness and oneness cannot be met through our ordinary ways of thinking. It must be constantly approached through the practice of virtue and contemplative ascent beyond the typical mental processes we use for other kinds of learning and knowing. If we are fortunate and worthy, we can recognize that Divine Providence is bestowing the Light we seek in some measure. If we are wise, we can accept that gift humbly and respectfully. If we are good and loving, we can joyfully put that Light to use not only for our own benefit, but to help better the lives of others and the world, and thereby facilitate the realization of more peace, harmony, and unity for everyone and everything.

DESTRUCTION AND REBUILDING

The central myth or traditional history of the Craft Lodge is focused on the building of King Solomon's Temple, also called the

First Temple. As addressed in various rites and rituals beyond the Master Mason Degree, the First Temple was destroyed and a Second Temple, also known as Herod's Temple, was built at the same location. The Second Temple was eventually ruined as well, and in some of our rites there are comments about the construction of a future Third Temple, sometimes explained as spiritual or metaphysical in nature, not a physical edifice.

There is a pattern here that began even before the First Temple with the Tabernacle, the tent that served as a movable sanctum while the people of Israel made their journey to the Promised Land. The pattern begins with disassembly or destruction, which is eventually followed by reassembly or reconstruction. This pattern can serve as a very rich and illuminating analogy for certain experiences in contemplative life, perhaps especially among mystics. The key to understanding this analogy is given to us in the First Degree, where we are taught that the lodge is not only a reflection of the Temple and thus also of the Tabernacle, but it is also a model for our own *"moral and Masonic edifice."* Note that the traditional language in many jurisdictions explicitly states this building project is both moral *and* Masonic, suggesting that it is not *only* moral, at least as morality is commonly understood. Rather, it is emphatically Masonic, and within the present context that means it is also contemplative and mystical.

In the following paragraphs, we proceed through three general phases – destruction, interregnum, and reconstruction. The term *interregnum* has been chosen to signify a pause, because its Latin roots allude to times between more overtly evident reigns of order. There is an inexhaustible quarry of potential insights in this analogy for any Mason's contemplative labors, and we will only trace some initial lines for now. As you proceed, it is helpful to grasp that these phases are not rigid steps, and so the sequencing of various elements may not always align exactly as they are given here.

DESTRUCTION

During their arduous sojourn through the wilderness, the Israelites constructed the Tabernacle as a portable shrine for the artifacts that facilitated their covenant and communion with the Creator. While tradition does not tell us that the Tabernacle was ever destroyed and rebuilt like the Temple, its repeated disassembly was certainly associated with great hardship. To begin with, the followers of Moses were made to wander in the wilderness for forty years before they were worthy to enter the Promised Land. Their nomadic existence was a consequence of the fear and rebellion that arose among them when they heard that the Promise Land's occupants were giants. Some of them even preferred to return to bondage in Egypt. As they roamed the desert, the Tabernacle had to frequently be taken down between resting places, and then set back up to fulfill its religious functions. After their entry into the Promised Land, the Tabernacle was at the center of various power struggles, was moved to new locations numerous times, was even separated from its most important furnishing, the Ark of the Covenant, and was apparently destroyed forever when God laid waste to Shiloh for its people's wickedness. By contrast, the First and Second Temples were plundered and destroyed by invading armies. Still, there is a common thread running through all these stories. According to the Tanakh, all these adversities were associated with the nation of Israel not trusting God's prophets or properly understanding and following God's laws.

In popular religion, these tales are frequently taken as allegories for what can happen when one strays too far from the prescriptions of religious authorities and their interpretations of scripture. Without arguing that idea, we instead apply the allegorical key previously mentioned. Thus, we find these accounts illustrative of a necessary experience in mystical realization, the destruction of the self-image, which may also be referred to as the disintegration of the persona and ego death.

When we are asleep in the illusion of separation, primarily ruled by desires and passions, our cultural and unconscious biases, and not attending much to the internal dimensions of our being, these challenges to the personality can seem like usurpers, intruders, invaders. They appear as if from some warring tribe, or even a foreign land, to suddenly attack the familiar structure and furnishings of our lives, forcing us into opportunities to question how we might have brought them on ourselves. We may or may not recognize or take advantage of such openings to self-inquiry, but if we do not, then we are bound to eventually wander into new yet very similar circumstances. If we do recognize them, we can more willingly welcome them and allow ourselves to begin letting go of that which no longer adequately serves our potentials and aspirations for mystical realization. This is the step of contemplative awareness that can make way for development of new understandings and more intentional manifestations of unity, wholeness, and harmony.

INTERREGNUM

After each disassembly of the Tabernacle, the Israelites wandered in search of a new temporary home. Similarly, between the destructions and resurrections of the Temple, they experienced times of collective dissolution and disarray in which there was much soul-searching, trying to understand how such a tragedy occurred and what would be necessary to make things right. With these cycles involving the Tabernacle and the Temple alike, the solution to their problems lies not only in the ordinary discursive processes of problem-solving, but in their openness to Divine guidance. With the Tabernacle, that guidance was given through Shekinah, the immanent presence of God leading them as a pillar of smoke by day and a pillar of flame by night. Furthermore, regarding the interregnums of the Temple, the inspirations and revelations of prophets were revisited during these interludes, including their warnings or explanations of how the nation and its leadership had lost the way by arrogantly and foolishly disregarding their spirituality and therefore losing harmony with the Divine and among themselves. The prophets' admonitions for a better relationship with the One and each other included a return to humility and service to God and their neighbors with faith, hope, and love.

From a contemplative and mystical point of view, this interregnum phase corresponds to the soul searching each of us does when reflecting upon the crumbled self-image that was one's personal temple. At the onset, an interregnum commonly includes some if not all the elements of both grief and trauma, such as shock, disbelief, pain, anger, acceptance, sadness, remorse, confusion, disorganization, and anxiety about the future. These conditions may lead into careful review of the destruction experience as well as the factors contributing to it, which aids in identifying what can be learned from it. There is also often a thoughtful inventory of what remains in the aftermath, consideration of what hindsight indicates as faulty or lacking, attempts to discern what is worth repairing and preserving, and the emergence of possibilities for how things could be different.

As suggested by the sagas of the Tabernacle and the Temple, the dim interregnum of the self is also a time when we can, whether instinctively or with knowing intention, humbly seek more light. We might turn to scripture, the words of philosophers and poets, and the testimonies of those who have gone this way before us. It is quite common to revisit things that are already familiar to us and have perhaps become taken for granted, but are now rediscovered with new eyes and ears to see and hear subtleties and depths of wisdom that had previously eluded us. We, like the Israelites, may also sense that, beyond the veils of our thoughts and feelings, an intelligent presence observes and offers guidance, is sometimes heard speaking to us through a "still small voice" of prophetic wisdom, and perhaps even intervenes to help us on the quest for mystical realization.

This development is very common in the patterns of contemplative life, and we find it addressed in similar but not identical ways across various traditions – Spirit Guide, Personal Daimon, Higher Self, Holy Guardian Angel, etc. For some people, this presence may even be related to in a less intermediary way as the voice or hand of God. In any case, it is evidence of the personality's recognition of its limitations and the need for and prayerful openness to intuition and inspiration from a mysterious source beyond personal awareness and control, yet a source which is nonetheless intimately interconnected with one's being – it is both integral and external. It marks a new, or *re-newed*, way of being in which the ordinary barriers between one's personal self, others, and the Great Mystery are more permeable, and there is greater lucidity of the Mystic Tie amid the apparent duality of our otherness.

As the reflection, inventory, and re-awakening of this phase coalesces, one develops a reconstituted awareness of how various strengths, weaknesses, values, interests, and opportunities uniquely intersect within one's life. In other words, there is more clarity about what one needs and has to offer in the quest for greater realization of unity, wholeness, and harmony. Also, in sensing the guidance and influence of a transpersonal source of wisdom, one may perceive a more particular feeling of responsibility, a mission or calling, not only for one's own benefit, but in loving service to others and the Absolute. Thus, a new self-image begins to form, like designs for a new personal temple being drawn on the tracing board of one's imagination.

RECONSTRUCTION

With the construction of the First Temple, it was meant to be a more beautiful, awe-inspiring, and enduring house than the Tabernacle for communing with the living presence of God, and a more suitable home for the sacred artifacts most worthy of passing on to future generations. Interestingly, while the Temple had been the dream of King David and the project of his son Solomon, and thus a distinctly Jewish religious edifice, both scripture and Masonic tradition assert that it could not have been built without the help of Gentiles. Most notable of these are King Hiram of Tyre and his workers, who worshipped the Divine in the form of Melqart, the Phoenician Ba'al. Furthermore, in the Book of Isaiah, the Temple had been ordained by God as a "house of prayer for all the nations." We can see this inclusive ideal manifest in the Masonic lodge, where Masons of different faiths, cultures, ethnicities, and nationalities join in prayer side-by-side. The reconstruction project that produced the Second Temple was guided by the same intentions as the First Temple and with the backing of the Persian kings Cyrus the Great and Darius I, neither of whom practiced Judaism, and both of whom were not only tolerant but actively supported people of various religions.

By analogy, we may take the stories of the Temple's completed construction and reconstruction as allusions to the wholeness and harmony of the Mystic Tie. They can also be understood as speaking to our mission as Masons to make each of our own lives not only a more beautiful, well furnished, and enduring temple, but also one that welcomes others, at least in toleration, as living extensions of the One. Additionally, the reality of impermanence is an obvious theme, reminding us that no self-image and no manifestation of our personal being will ever be established as permanent and unchanging, even one reflecting deep awareness and understanding of its own illusoriness. The world changes, contexts change, and because it is interconnected with the All, the self is always changing through its experiences in space and time. So, the self-image must either be knowingly and willingly adjusted with those conditions, or it becomes increasingly false, in friction with the greater reality of the whole self, and fragile. As contemplative mystics, we aim to moderate these follies and the painfully tragic dramas they create by embracing the cycle of destruction, interregnum, and reconstruction with awareness and understanding.

On that note, we suggest that there is another traditional story that reflects this same pattern, and we will review that mystery somewhat obscurely except to those who have ears to hear. There was once a very good man, highly competent as an adept of many arts and sciences, who was the master of a very important project. Yet, all his virtue, knowledge, and skill did not prevent his violent demise before the project could be completed. He was a human being who did not foresee or have the power to quell the triple threat that would waylay him.

Overlaid with his mythic destruction is that of many others who have emulated him by symbolically making a willing sacrifice of their old lives. As each such substitute has lain silently waiting in the darkness of ignorance, uncertainty, and powerlessness, a voice of wisdom has been heard speaking of the inevitability of this experience and of what can and cannot lift one up to a state of renewal and readiness to carry on the work. Only after a remembrance and invocation of the Divine is the substitute able to ascend by the assistance of others and be recognized as the most recent reiteration of every potential represented by the original master of the project. This new adept is then presented with all the tools necessary for the project, with emphasis on one. Life is no longer merely about oneself, no longer led by the illusion of separation into deeper layers of conflict with self and others. Now there is a calling to continually seek the truth that is every soul's Divine essence, repeatedly dying and being reborn to greater lucidity and harmony with that infinite essence, and thus be empowered to work with the cement of the Mystic Tie more intentionally and joyfully.

CONCLUSION

If this chapter serves no other purpose, then let it speak to you of the oneness, wholeness, and harmony you might find in knowing that all the challenges and rewards in contemplative life have been and are now being known by others, and they will be known by others yet to come. Not only are you not alone, but you are also participating in the perennial dance of parts of the All re-awakening to union with the One. That dance has recognizable movements, like designs on a cosmic trestleboard, and knowingly and willingly moving through those patterns is vital to the way of oneness, of true initiation and the quest for mystical realization.

INITIATION

Awakening in the night's dark midst,
From dreamless sleep we hear a call.
Then wrapped in silent deep blue mist
We pass into an ancient hall.

About us hung in golden frames,
And peering from mosaic tiles,
Loom kindred faces lit by flames
Reflected in their knowing smiles.

Around the crown in bas relief
Are carved their mythic memories,
Their wars and quests, their joy and grief,
Their treks across the sapphire seas.

Great sacrifices they have made,
Preparing this old hallowed place,
Securing with both love and blade
This Temple filled with art and grace.

Through adytum and portico
Soft voices echo from each wall.
The epic songs from muses flow
That eons hence we'll still recall.

Those mortals from the Earth's damp sod,
Their fruitful legends now grown ripe,
Have each transformed into a god,
The icon of an archetype.

Within their gaze we cross the floor
To pursue our spirits' mission.
Past azure veils a pearly door
Guards the font of all tradition.

With simple faith we strike the knocks
That sound the driven seekers' plea.
With thunderous quakes the cosmic locks
Shake down each soul to bended knee.

The portal opens with a knell
Into the depths of virgin space,
And here dumbfounded we must dwell
Upon an ageless profiled Face.

There from its clear Eternal Eye
A cascade of light comes streaming;
As from a prism bright rays fly,
To illuminate God's dreaming.

Now on this rainbow span of light
We find our fitting harmonies,
Wherein our flames of will ignite
And dance upon the heavenly breeze.

Then drawn within the dazzling swell,
We let the current carry us
Back toward where our sparks once fell,
Though now with renewed consciousness.

Returning through our heroes' shrine,
We sense the rally of their souls,
And joining with their lodge divine
Our names are added to its rolls.

Beneath the brightest of all moons,
Across the mighty banks of time,
They pass to us their greatest boons
That we may do the Work Sublime.

So, exiting our Sanctum's porch,
Once more upon our odysseys,
We bear with us a sacred torch,
A mystic word and magic keys.

Now sailing back through night's black mist,
As the Great Architect so deems,
We stir in morning's amethyst
To rise awake in daylight dreams.

CHAPTER EIGHT
LIVING WITH A MYSTICAL PERSPECTIVE

In this closing chapter, we summarize and expand on ideas from previous chapters by examining the important role of perspective for a life of greater unity, wholeness, and harmony. When we speak of perspective in physical terms, we mean the position in space from which one views other things, such as how far away one is, how high or low, and features of the territory between oneself and a focal point. Perspective is an ever-present fact to which our minds automatically respond in forming our perceptions. From different physical perspectives, the same material object can be seen very differently, and its viewers may even come to contrary conclusions about what the object is. When it comes to how we think and feel about less tangible things, perspectives include the beliefs, values, memories, education, and mental habits that form the meanings we give to our experiences. Each of these factors has an influence on how we understand and react to what we perceive. For example, the same public event, legislative action, or judicial ruling can be interpreted in conflicting ways by political partisans of the left and right, while persons on each side are fully convinced of the validity of their own conclusions. From their particular perspectives, their understandings and reactions make good sense, as they do to others who share similar perspectives, while seeming like nonsense to people with very different perspectives.

Having similar physical perspectives affords people similar sensory experiences of the world, which makes it easier to reach agreements about what they are dealing with and how to deal with it. To do so, people can usually change their position in space, thereby adjusting their vantage point and arriving at a shared perspective. With matters not limited to the physical dimension – religion, politics, ethics, and many other things – such shifts can be considerably more challenging. Even so, for people to function together in peace and harmony there must be a sufficient degree of commonality among their differing perspectives. Those people who are most successful in experiencing and facilitating peace, harmony, and unity in the world are also those people most skillful in adjusting their own perspectives, at least temporarily, or who have a perspective that is inclusive of as many other perspectives as possible.

For anyone on the way of oneness, the need to become more lucid and intentional with perspective is especially important. Mystical experiences typically undermine the views most of us have been taught by our cultures, and thus they demand that we develop new views that better account for the insights we receive. As a new perspective is developed, if we are to function in greater unity, wholeness, and harmony with others and even within ourselves, then that perspective must also account for and be accommodating of non-mystical perspectives while not entirely reverting to them in neglect or denial of the light we have received.

From the time we are born, most of us are immersed in the consensus views that existence is fundamentally fragmented, oppositional, and threatening, and that our only hope for liberation is either removed from us in some far away heaven or in a supposed total and permanent loss of awareness at death. This convention is built up and reinforced through hour after hour of conditioning, assumptions, and messages based on the illusion of separation. Conforming to this "common sense" perspective leads us to develop layers of mental, emotional, and physical habits that intersect with countless psychological, spiritual, and social maladies. These vices and superfluities on the ashlars of our souls distract us from self-awareness and lucidity, keep us stuck in false dichotomies, and frustrate our natural desires for wholeness, harmony, and unity. Indeed, the consensus view of existence can be a dazzling ornate veil between us and greater awareness of our true nature in the Mystic Tie. It is no wonder that many mystics have chosen paths of radical renunciation to abandon more ordinary lifestyles and even retreat into entirely cloistered lives. The world has benefited by those who have chosen such paths, and it will continue to do so.

As respectable as they are, such ways of withdrawal are not what the Builder's Art upholds for its initiates. Masonry responds to these problems by encouraging us to enjoy fellowship with people of diverse backgrounds and identities and with differing religious and political views, refine our self-awareness, develop universally respected virtues, contemplate the wonders of nature, become competent in the Liberal Arts and Sciences, and practice sincere compassion, generosity, and loving kindness with all. These practices are meant to empower

Masons to be active and engaged workers in the temple of society, not only the temple of our own souls. Such pursuits are indeed critical to the cohesiveness of society, but they are not unique to our tradition.

Seeing no more substance than these simple elements of civility, people are sometimes led to conclude that the Craft offers nothing to warrant its vast symbolic array of emblems, elaborate ceremonies, solemn vows of secrecy, noble titles, and majestic regalia. However, this conclusion usually fails to give due attention to two further points: (1) the Mystic Tie is not just a fraternal feeling or even a formally declared sense of obligation, and (2) the Master Mason has a continuing charge to seek Light and the Lost Word. As we have seen in previous chapters, these two points reveal the non-sectarian mystical aspirations of our institution that most distinguish it from others. In short, the Builder's Art regards mysticism as central to the most optimal perspective for peace, harmony, and unity in our lives as individuals and together in community; that is the "vital spark" and "secret strength" of Masonry mentioned by Brother Claudy in his poem, "The Road," cited in Chapter 1. Every traditional emblem, allegory, and instrument of the Craft has the potential to capture some portion of our attention and energy and direct it in accord with that perspective. If we ignore those potentials, then we allow our lodges to be ruled instead by profane ways of thinking and give credibility to the critique of Masonry as a ridiculously ostentatious ego-stroking institution.

All the practices presented in this book are useful for helping us attain mystical realization, especially when applied as a whole. Even so, the profane world's everyday onslaught of falsehoods and distractions rarely subsides, and so it is quite understandable that our lucidity and loving expression of oneness can be difficult to develop and hard to consistently maintain. Ideally speaking, this is where our fraternal experiences of the Mystic Tie and our shared commitment to seek the Lost Word are of the greatest value. When a lodge is duly opened and attended by brothers holding a mystical perspective, we create a sacred space in which to remember the immanent presence of the Great Architect of the Universe, not only around us but within ourselves and each other. The lodge meeting thus becomes a time and place set aside for experiencing what social existence can be like when we are lovingly mindful of oneness, even amid activities as commonplace as paying bills or having a meal. In this environment, the Mystic Tie manifests as a union of hearts and minds supporting each other to develop greater resilience in recognizing and responding from a mystical perspective to the demands of the profane world and all its illusions and distractions. Furthermore, our rituals' repeated admonitions to seek the Lost Word and our reflective dialogues about its meaning, serve as inspiring affirmations that there is indeed something supremely worthwhile to be more fully realized by maintaining and acting in accord with a mystical view on life. At the very least, our lodge activities can demonstrate that we are not alone in our mystical quest, and the memory of that communion can help sustain a mystical perspective while we are involved in our usual vocations.

When our contemplative practices and fraternal experiences are infused with a mystical perspective, they provide us with the designs and tools for that perspective to be employed in the world around us. All philosophical perspectives rest upon certain axioms, which are postulates or suppositions taken at the start to be fundamentally true and from which everything else in that perspective should logically follow. So, among the mystic's most valuable tools is critical thinking, which makes good use of the third step on the Fellow Craft's staircase, the art of Logic. This art enables us to question, analyze, and better discern the degree of truth or falsehood in every aspect of common sense that we have been taught and, perhaps unconsciously, adopted as our own. More specifically, critical thinking facilitates our recognition and understanding of how such views may rest upon and perpetuate the illusion of separation as axiomatic, and it can facilitate insight about how they contribute to confusion and suffering that would otherwise be unnecessary.

Another significant value in critical thinking is that it can help us be more aware of how our mystical views might lack grounding, be too heavily interwoven with spiritual glamor, ego defense, or superstition, or unwisely include denial of the great value in this diverse experience of creation. Regarding that last possibility, it is a sad yet repeated tale that some mystics are in frequent hostile conflict with the prevailing consensus, may even become embittered with feelings of estrangement, and thereby neglect the wisdom, strength, and beauty that can be experienced and expressed among people who do not share their perspective. Of course, the best intention in this resistance to society's norms is to remain lucid and keep the focus on oneness, but that intention is misguided when it is too busy decrying so much of the One's self-manifestation in the All, even in those people and things that seem to block our paths; it thus fails to welcome some measure of the Mystic Tie's wholeness. Mutually beneficial coexistence with people who do not share our perspective is analogous to different voices singing in harmony, where all voices are not singing the same notes and perhaps not at the same time, but they can still complement each other in the wholeness of beautiful music. Critical thinking can help maintain and refine our mystical perspective as we dissolve our self-defeating self-contradictions, and especially the self-imposed barriers that prevent us from harmonizing our lives through a more unconditional embrace of the One in everyone and everything.

Perhaps by now it is understood that such an embrace does not mean total capitulation, complacency, and conformity with the many ills of our world. Neither is a genuine mystical perspective pollyannish nor aggressively reactionary. Rather, it aims to witness and respond to all the world's confusion and suffering without the highly filtered, narrowly constrained perspectives and automatic reactions that are typical when we are driven by enculturated biases, ego defense mechanisms, unresolved past trauma, and the stress of overcomplicated lifestyles. To meet and respond to life more lucidly, intentionally, and holistically requires not only openness to intuition, inspiration, and critical thinking, but also empathy and compassion. Harmonious integration of these spiritual, intellectual, and emotional factors nurtures awareness and understanding of our interconnectedness, and thus we are enabled to act in more virtuous ways and to better facilitate the most beautiful and joyful potentials of the Mystic Tie.

> *In the Ecology of Oneness, you develop a deep understanding and appreciation that you do not have to be the same as or in lockstep with the various others with whom you share your vision, but rather that each contributes consciously and compassionately to the Whole in the best possible way they know how, individually and collectively. (Robert Sachs, The Ecology of Oneness)*

Again and again it behooves us to return to the Principal Tenets, the Theological Virtue of Charity, and the Master Mason's Trowel, or in a single word, *love*, the crowning jewel of the Builder's Art. Without knowing and sharing love in such positive forms, one cannot truly have a mystical perspective. Love is what leads us to contemplatively seek the One within the center of ourselves and to manifest the wholeness of our being more fully, not only for our benefit but for others. In devotion to the Great Mystery, love is what guides us to reach outward to embrace the whole circle of the One's self-expression in the Mystic Tie. When encountering all others in this magnificent tapestry of existence, love is what facilitates recognition and harmonization of our interconnectedness, and thus draws us back to the shared thread of oneness within each and all. Within a mystical perspective, all our Masonic fraternal activities, every contemplative practice, and every virtue can be known as experiences and expressions of love for the non-dimensional point of the One *and* the multidimensional circle of everything that It begets from Itself, including one's own personal being. Thus, when we struggle with holding a mystical perspective, when our lucidity wanes and our sight is obscured by the veil of consensus views, or when the defunct temple of our self-image lies in ruins, even in these moments, thinking and acting intentionally in love for the Divine, for others, and for ourselves, can keep us on the way of oneness and deliver us into greater wholeness, harmony, and unity with the Mystic Tie.

In that light, a parting poem is offered.

A TOAST TO THE BROTHERS OF THE MYSTIC TIE

Now hark you brothers of the Mystic Tie
And join this toast with glasses high!

Say your cheers to fraternity
And share the wine of charity,
For many a gift we now behold
Will slip away as we grow old.

Our worldly tools we'll set aside
That once we held with manly pride.
All that seems so sharp today
Will in due time just rust away.

And for each brother, O so dear,
Too soon will come a parting tear,

So, look about our table now,
And share with all a solemn bow.

Now hark you brothers of the Mystic Tie
And for this toast keep glasses high!

These words aren't meant to cast a gloom,
Or bring death's chill into the room,
But to remind us of the Light
That shines eternal, clear, and bright.
The Master Builder has so deemed
That in our souls a beacon beams,
A spark immortal from the flame
In which He writes His Holy Name.

Let's light our smiles now with that fire
To which all mystics should aspire,
And know the joy our Master knows
When in our hearts His pure love glows.

Now drink you brothers of the Mystic Tie
And share this cup with spirits high!

AFTERWORD
EMBRACING THE MYSTIC TIE AND
THE WAY OF ONENESS

BY RT. WOR. BARUTI KMT-SISOUVONG, PHD, 32°

During my sojourn through Graduate School at Maharishi International University in Fairfield, Iowa USA and at the early stage of what would later come to inform my Doctoral Dissertation research, I was graciously granted the opportunity to visit the Guthrie Scottish Rite Library in Guthrie, Oklahoma, USA by Most Worshipful Robert G. Davis, 33°, GC, PGM in 2010. In hindsight, it was the opportunity that would energize my intellectual development as it relates to Freemasonry and the depth of the lessons encoded within our beloved and varied rituals. Seemingly as if by design of the Great Architect of the Universe, it was during the weekend of research and discussion, that I had the pleasure of meeting and connecting with one whom I came to view as a "confessional scholar" as it relates to the hidden beauties of Craft ritual—Brother Chuck Dunning, 33°. As a relatively new Mason, having been raised the evening of Tuesday, 18 August 2009 in Fairfield, the research trip was an experience that would come to inform me Masonically in countless ways along the path. Over the years, as a result of that weekend's many exchanges, Brother Dunning and I have collaborated on several occasions with lasting results for the projects in which we engaged and for, I suspect, us as brothers.

As a result of our longstanding success in collaborating on projects over the years, when Chuck approached me to pen the afterword for the book you now read, it was not long after my having successfully defended my doctoral dissertation research on mystical experiences among Freemasons, I agreed with great enthusiasm. In contacting me, it seems the invisible chain linking both he and I and our respective research interests and endeavours together in an indissoluble connection once again opted to show itself. With yet another opportunity to collaborate, at least in my mind's-eye, our respective journeys are not unlike the double-helix strand of deoxyribonucleic acid (DNA) which intersects at key points and maintains the integrity of the molecule and, in so doing, the superstructure of which it is an integral component. Here we are collaborating yet again.

Like many of you, over the years, I have read, studied, and thoroughly enjoyed Brother Dunning's sagacious offerings to our hearts and minds as they relate to the beauty of the Craft, the ritual, our brethren, our lodges, and what they represent — their divinely contemplative nature. As a result, it is an honour to share a few thoughts on his latest work as it beautifully articulates the possibilities of inner and outer transformation for those daring to peer below the surface of our rituals and inner reality to plumb new depths of available understanding for action as we travel within the Universal Lodge.

Reflecting on Chuck Dunning's profound offering within *The Mystic Tie and the Way of Oneness*, we are reminded of the deep and ever-present connections that bind us all into one common mass — transcending the boundaries of individuality and bringing us face-to-face with our collective unity. As a result, we rejoice in the reality of both our unique individuality and fundamentally unified aspects. As a scholar within the discipline of Vedic Science and Certified Teacher of Transcendental Meditation, along with serving as Director of the program within Cambridge and Metropolitan Boston, my journey has long been one of bridging ancient wisdom with modern scientific inquiry while simultaneously seeking to experience and understand the very fabric of Consciousness and the varied pathways to personal and collective growth — perpetually. In the first instance from my research, we observed and posit that by incorporating a meditative or contemplative practice as part of one's daily studies of rituals within Freemasonry, the depths of beauty contained therein surface more readily in ways perhaps not previously considered. In short, if approached with an open heart and mind, Masonic ritual possesses the possibility of impacting one for many decades to come after one's initial experience as a candidate knocking upon the door with three distinct knocks.

As for the ways ritual may be experienced, from our research, we note five material ways ritual (symbolized by the asterisk at the center of the below figure) may be experienced — as a candidate; as a brother delivering the ritual i.e., a ritualist; as a sideline brother witnessing the ritual; as one contemplates the ritual away from a tyled Lodge in the privacy of one's Internal Lodge or mind; and by living it in one's daily travels. From these experiences a deeper sense of understanding emerges related to the Craft itself.

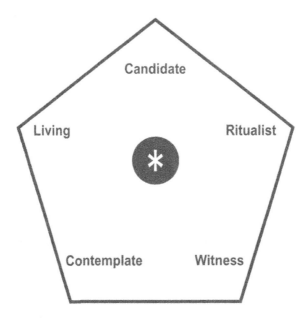

Reflecting upon the preceding figure from our research, readers will quickly recognize the points of connection with Brother Dunning's offering. Thus, we anticipate a renewed understanding of not only the import of our various rituals and the ways, as articulated above, those rituals may be experienced, but also the ways we are called to live the lessons contained therein for the betterment of each of us and the several stations wherein we travel along our journey. As current and future academics, researchers, and authors delve into that which may be wrought by intentional encounters with masonic ritual in the ways suggested by Brother Dunning, we will come to embrace the intersection of mysticism and modern science as it relates to the Craft with yet untold beneficial outcomes for all concerned.

We also note that the concept of the Mystic Tie as presented by Chuck aligns beautifully with the principles of Vedic Science as developed by Maharishi Mahesh Yogi, my chosen area of research. Both emphasize the interconnectedness of all life and the potential for experiencing and ultimately living what Maharishi posits as higher states of consciousness. In that vein, my research has shown that by contemplating the lessons present within Masonic ritual, individuals can experience profound shifts in awareness, leading to mystical experiences that provide subsequently greater clarity, creativity, and inner peace. These experiences are not merely esoteric; they have tangible benefits for mental and physical health, as supported by a growing body of scientific evidence. If my soon-to-be-tested theory holds, incorporating practices such as Transcendental Meditation into Masonic curriculum, one may be shown to advance yet further and faster along this perfecting path, or as I like to refer to it from my research, *The Model for Perpetual Growth and Progress*.

Central to my work is the *Model for Perpetual Growth and Progress*, a practical and an actionable framework that outlines a continuous journey of self-improvement in the direction of enlightenment. The model resonates with the themes of unity and wholeness discussed in Brother Dunning's book and illustrates that growth is not a linear process but an ongoing cycle of expansion, integration, and actions where each step forward deepens our understanding of ourselves, our place within the universe, and the yet-to-be discovered ways we may successfully contribute to our collective human enterprise in a more meaningful manner. By embracing and engaging the *Model for Perpetual Growth and Progress*, I posit we will cultivate a mindset of lifelong learning and development, continually striving to align with our highest potential. Such is akin to Carol Dweck, PhD and her work with the growth mindset (2019).

With this mindset and our journey through Craft ritual safely deposited within our hearts, with all the experiences of the lessons of the Blue Lodge as well as the Scottish Rite (Southern Jurisdiction), we posit that beneficial results may be observed in all one's thoughts, words, deeds, and outcomes, as they ripple out into the Universal Lodge for the benefit of all.

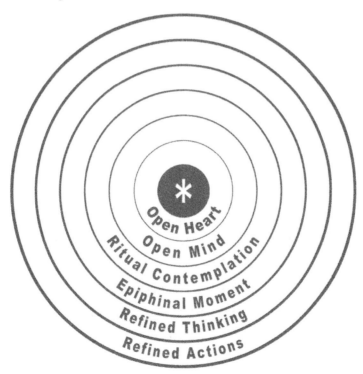

In reflecting upon my academic and personal journey to comprehend unity and wholeness, I have witnessed the transformative power of recognizing and nurturing the Mystic Tie, both on an individual basis as well as within small groups. As educators, researchers, and practitioners, we have a responsibility to foster environments that support holistic well-being. This involves not only intellectual growth but also emotional, spiritual, and by logical extension, social development. By creating spaces that honor the interconnected nature of human existence, despite social constructs that seek to have us remain at a perpetual distance, we can inspire others to embark on their own journeys of self-discovery toward an understanding of fundamental unity. In so doing, as my then Dissertation Advisor, Fred Travis, PhD, often fondly remarked, "You don't merely experience Being, you *become* Being." In so becoming, a formidable cornerstone is laid for future directions in Consciousness research. Something close to my heart and work.

As I look toward the future of the Craft while reflecting upon the famous passage from Foster Bailey in his work titled *The Spirit of Masonry,*

> *Great as Masonry has been in the past, it has before it a still more glorious and useful future as it moves from the Speculative to Spiritual Masonry. That inevitable change is already dimly seen. It will be more important than the change from Operative to Speculative Masonry. It is towards this end that Masonic research should direct its efforts (1957, p. 146)*

I am compelled to contend that with Chuck's latest offering, alongside my own research to be fully shared within forthcoming works, future generations coming to Freemasonry will discover that the rich tapestry of our ritual is ever a balm for the journey of inner exploration and outer growth, and ever connected to the Mystic Tie. In short, the future of Masonic research coupled with an understanding of and direct experience with the Mystic Tie — or in Vedic Science parlance, Pure Consciousness or the Transcendent — holds immense promise for those yet to knock upon the door of the lodge. For example, advances in neuroimaging and psychophysiology offer new avenues for exploring the effects of meditation and other contemplative practices on the brain and body. Collaborative efforts between scientists and Masonic contemplative practitioners can lead to deeper insights into the mechanisms underlying higher states of consciousness and even the outcomes of deeply contemplating Masonic ritual. Furthermore, integrating these findings into educational and organizational settings, where Freemasons have historically held positions of influence, can enhance overall well-being and productivity, fostering a culture of mindfulness and compassion which, undoubtedly, holds great promise in the areas of practical applications and broader implications.

The practical implications of understanding and experiencing the Mystic Tie, or Pure Consciousness, are vast. In educational settings, incorporating mindfulness and meditation can enhance focus, reduce stress, and improve academic performance. In the corporate world, these practices can lead to more harmonious workplaces, increased creativity, and better decision-making. On a societal level, fostering a sense of interconnectedness as a result of one's stable connection with Pure Consciousness can promote greater empathy, reduce national and international conflict, and encourage sustainable living. As we continue to explore these applications, we move closer to realizing a world where the principles of unity and wholeness are fully embraced. Those Masons serving in positions of influence, consciously cultivating their understanding of and connection to Pure Consciousness, serve as a point of Light in this regard. Imagine, if you will, what more can emerge from the minds of those so practiced. The possibilities for our collective advancement are endless.

In conclusion, the journey toward a deep understanding of Brother Dunning's offering discussing *The Mystic Tie and the Way of Oneness* is one that aligns deeply with both my research and personal philosophy. By integrating ancient wisdom with modern science, we can unlock latent potentials for personal and collective growth. Therefore, this book serves as a testament to the timeless quest for unity, offering insights and practices that can guide us on our path. As we move forward, let us remain committed to fostering environments that nurture the whole person, be they personal or professional, thus recognizing that in our acknowledged and acted upon interconnectedness lies the true essence of humanity — fundamental unity.

Finally, I am deeply grateful to Brother Chuck Dunning for inviting me to contribute to this work. His exploration of the Mystic Tie provides a rich tapestry of insights that resonate with my own journey and research in beautiful ways and illustrates a thread that seems to have connected us before we actually met in Guthrie, Oklahoma all those years ago. Therefore, it is my fervent desire that this afterword will inspire readers to delve further into their own understanding of unity and wholeness, to deeply study our Mystic Tie, and to thereby fully embrace the journey of perpetual growth and progress with an open heart and a curious mind. In so doing, it is my considered belief that each of us will leave the world a little bit better than when we entered from the great unknown and prepare to travel to that undiscovered country once again.

Baruti KMT-Sisouvong, PhD,
PDDGM, 32°
Cambridge, MA
June 13, 2024

APPENDIX
DEVELOPING MYSTICAL INTERPRETATIONS OF MASONIC SYMBOLS

Various interpretations of Masonic symbols have been offered in this book. However, it has also been repeatedly asserted that interpretation and application of the Craft's symbols is a responsibility we each bear. Our rituals present us with starting places, and with those as our shared foundation, we are encouraged to continue contemplating for more light. Just as examining a flower in different kinds of light – the visible spectrum, infrared, and ultraviolet – tells us more about that flower, so there are also different lights for interpretation. Following the approach of the Masonic Legacy Society, we can consider how a symbol sheds light on either the physical, emotional, or intellectual aspects of our lives.[12] That approach can also develop interpretations that are primarily relevant to (1) the Internal Lodge, our own psychospiritual being, (2) the External Lodge, our fraternal settings and experiences, or (3) the Universal Lodge, including but not limited to the workings of nature and sociopolitical matters. These are all fitting, fruitful, and complementary pursuits, while the central point of this book is about following the way of oneness for greater realization of unity, wholeness, and harmony with the Mystic Tie, the mysterious interconnectedness of all that is with its Creator.

12. Learn more about the Masonic Legacy Society at https://masoniclegacysociety2026.com/.

Keep in mind that once you have a mystical interpretation for a symbol you are not then done with it. Every symbol is capable of being the catalyst for many new insights and facilitating deep and mysterious changes in one's soul throughout one's life. In this regard, contemplating symbols is analogous to eating and drinking, and we willingly partake of many of the same foods and beverages repeatedly throughout our lives. The processes of dining can be very meaningful and enjoyable not only as a personal experience but also socially as part of our bonding with others. At an unconscious level, food and drink is also very importantly being digested and nutrients released to support the various organs and systems of the body. To engage the analogous processes with Masonic symbols, the following method is recommended.

1. Choose a Masonic symbol as a focal point. This might be any particular thing from a traditional trestleboard, symbolic carpet, or collection of lecture slides, or words or actions in a ritual. Briefly recall or review any monitorial or ritual explanation of this symbol and/or the ways in which attention is traditionally drawn to it.

2. Take plenty of time to get comfortable, closing your eyes, breathing slow, full, peaceful breaths, relaxing deeply, and becoming still and quiet without any attempt to focus on the symbol. Focus on releasing tension from your body and becoming physically, emotionally, and mentally calm. This step is key to being more effective with those that follow. Give it time.

3. Invoke the aid of Deity, perhaps using some of the steps of mystical prayer as presented in Chapter 4. Specifically ask for assistance with developing mystical insight into the symbol.

4. For several minutes, focus your attention on the symbol while being open to whatever spontaneously arises about it. This step is more about allowing something to come to you than performing a systematic intellectual process. Without judgment or censure, just note whatever occurs. If you find yourself becoming distracted or following some tangent away from the focal point, then gently return to holding it at the center of your attention, knowing that you can do other kinds of thinking later.

5. When you are ready, offer a prayer of thanks, even if nothing meaningful seems to have come to you. It is important to recognize that something may well have happened outside your personal awareness that could emerge later.

6. Gently reground yourself in awareness of your physical senses, beginning with feeling, then hearing, and finally seeing with the opening of your eyes.

7. Make notes about what you experienced when focused on the symbol. Simply jot down a few words as reminders of what happened. Then begin to reflect on that experience and write whatever associations or possibilities of meaning it might hold for you.

8. Dig deeper into the mystical possibilities by pondering and recording how the focal point and whatever came to you could shed more light on these interrelated mysteries:

    a. Unity

    b. Wholeness

    c.   Harmony

    d.   The Mystic Tie, the Divine interconnectedness of all that is as well as its more particular manifestation in the sacred bond of Masonry

    e.   Love

9.   Discuss your insights with at least one other Mason who shares your interests, recognizing that the dialogue itself may facilitate further development of your interpretation.

10.   Be mindful of three reasons that the practice of mystical interpretation never truly ends:

    a.   Mystically speaking, symbols are finite ways through which we can develop further realization of the Infinite, thus many interpretations can have value while none can ever fully capture all that might be revealed.

    b.   As we continue to learn and grow, our interpretations can become more refined and nuanced, or even radically change.

    c.   Symbols affect not only our personal awareness but also the unconscious levels of our being.

GLOSSARY

Of Terms as They are Used in This Book

Archetypes: from the Greek for "principal forms," the metaphysical frameworks that provide the potentials for things observable with the physical senses; regarded by Plato and other mystics as more real than physical objects because they are eternal and unchanging whereas physical objects are only their temporary and changing expressions in space and time.

Awareness: a state of consciousness characterized by the ability to perceive and attend to things; discussed in Chapter 2 as the first in a three-step cycle of engaging a contemplative path.

Builder's Art: a term for Masonry highlighting its constructive and creative dimensions, its concern with beauty, and alluding to its aim to emulate the beautiful creativity of the Divine Builder.

Chant: the rhythmic repetition of a sound, word, phrase, or longer statement as part of a contemplative process like prayer or meditation; chanting helps focus the mind, eliminate distractions, and can stimulate psychophysiological effects by vibration and oxygenation; the thing to be repeated is often referred to by the Sanskrit word *mantra*, which means an "invocational formula."

Common Sense: a collection of behaviors, beliefs, and attitudes that are customarily shared and expected among the people of a given culture, facilitating their ability to coexist, cooperate, and collaborate, yet often so habitual as to contribute to a lifestyle of automatic reactivity with little awareness or understanding; presented in Chapter 3 as a central aspect of the Visible Realm in Plato's Divided Line.

Consensus View of Existence: a culture's dominant perspective about the nature of being, often unrecognized and unquestioned, giving rise to much of what is regarded as common sense; a nearly constant challenge for most people wanting to maintain a mystical perspective and lucidity, and yet one which mystical Masons must be able to accommodate to have a mutually beneficial presence in ordinary society.

Consciousness: the fundamental nature of mind, if not reality itself, with a range of potential states and functions, including wakefulness, dreaming, and dreamless sleep; spelled with a capital C, it becomes a Divine name denoting that God, Ultimate Reality, the Absolute, etc., can be related to as the transcendent yet all-pervading Mind.

Contemplation: the practice of intentional awareness by an individual or a group, which facilitates the ability to understand and manifest things; it includes the abilities to relax, reduce unwanted mental activity, concentrate, reason, empathize, and open to intuition and inspiration; various forms include meditation, mindfulness, prayer, reflection, and ritual; *contemplatives* are people for whom contemplation is a significant part of their lifestyle.

Craft: a name for Masonry emphasizing that it demands work and the development of specialized skills.

Destruction-Interregnum-Reconstruction: a three-phase pattern of personal transformation allegorically explained in Chapter 7 through the legends of the Tabernacle, the Temple, and a mythic role model.

Discursive Reasoning: explained in Chapter 3 as *dianoia*, the ability to use logic, especially in critical thinking, to better discern the truth or falseness of things; noted in Chapter 8 as useful in questioning common sense and consensus views, and thus for maintaining a mystical perspective; often held by modern thinkers as the pinnacle of human mental abilities but regarded by Plato as the entrance into the Intelligible Realm and surpassed by noesis.

Divine Name: any term representing That which is regarded as most sacred, true, or real; each such term expresses and emphasizes some aspect or quality of human experience by which we try to relate to That which nonetheless transcends experience and expression and thus remains mysterious; such terms typically have capitalized initial letters.

Duality: the perception of differences and oppositions characterized in binaries or groups of two, such as good and evil, masculine and feminine, light and darkness; *dualism* is a view in which duality is regarded as the fundamental quality of reality; by contrast, mysticism regards duality as an aspect of a single unified reality, and that all apparent binaries and oppositions are expressions of one underlying and/or all-encompassing truth.

Form of the Good: noted in Chapter 3 as Plato's term for the Supreme Archetype and the fundamental truth of all things, which can only be perceived through noesis.

Harmony: a pleasant integration of different yet interrelated things; one of the conditions traditionally held to characterize a well-functioning Masonic lodge, and thus also relevant to psychological, social, and spiritual well-being; a necessary aspect of more complete mystical realization.

Illusion: a misleading perception and/or understanding; mystically speaking, the fundamental illusion is that of separation, of complete disconnection from other beings and from That which is regarded as most sacred, true, or real, as discussed in Chapter 1.

Imagery: a process and product of the imagination; although commonly thought of in terms of visualizing objects and events in the mind, it can include imaginary perceptions analogous to any of the physical senses; many contemplative practices make intentional use of this faculty as well as opening the mind for the spontaneous stimulation of imagery from outside of personal awareness, which is the nature of visionary experience.

Initiation: a significant turning point marking an entry into a quest for personal transformation and mystical realization; it may or may not include a ceremonial aspect, but such is usually required in wisdom traditions like Masonry.

Inner Work: the active engagement in contemplative processes of self-inquiry, personal transformation, and mystical realization.

Intelligible Realm: as introduced on Plato's Divided Line in Chapter 3, levels of consciousness that have access to greater truth and archetypal reality than can be known through the physical senses and the common sense of cultural conditioning; it is entered through the faculty of dianoia and more fully known through noesis.

Intuition: a term commonly conflated with words like *assumption* and *hunch*, it classically refers to insight not arrived at through the physical senses, emotions, or ordinary thought processes, but by cognitive reception of something from beyond personal awareness.

Know Thyself: English for the Greek *gnothi seauton*; introduced in Chapter 3 as an ancient traditional admonition to seek self-awareness and self-understanding as the foundation for all other knowledge; often attributed to Pythagoras.

Love: a term broadly inclusive of all forms of human desire, attentiveness, affection, and care; an essential factor in mystical realization; in Masonry it is most clearly addressed through the Principal Tenets of

Brotherly Love, Relief, and Truth, the Theological Virtue of Charity (agape, universal spiritual love), and the working tool of the Trowel; spelled with a capital L, it refers to Divine Love, which transcends all our ordinary understandings and manifestations of love and its apparent oppositions such as apathy, fear, and hate.

Lucidity: a state of heightened awareness and clarity of understanding; regarding dreams, it is awareness that one is dreaming while the dream is occurring; in mysticism, it is awareness and understanding of the oneness, wholeness, and harmony of things while participating in the apparent otherness, fragmentation, and discord of ordinary life; it can be experienced across a range from less lucidity to more.

Manifestation: the observable expression of a potentiality, or the act of making something physically or socially evident; discussed in Chapter 2 as the third in a repeating three-step process of engaging a contemplative path.

Meditation: a process of mental focus and concentration, typically but not always including rhythmic breathing, relaxation, and being still and quiet; a key skill set for developing awareness and understanding.

Mindfulness: the practice of being as aware and accepting as possible of the immediately present moment, less distracted by expectations, judgments, making conclusions, or thoughts of the past or future; its practice helps with experiencing things more as they are, less filtered by bias and prejudice, and engaging in things with greater wholeness and harmony; a very important part of ritual as a contemplative practice.

Mysticism: the pursuit of realizing union with That which is regarded as most sacred, true, or real; a *mystical perspective* is a view that existence is in unity with That which is its transcendent source; a *mystic* is one who engages in practices aimed at maintaining a mystical perspective and developing mystical realization.

Mystery: something that seems enigmatic, elusive, esoteric, hidden, or difficult to observe or understand; in mysticism, the deeper metaphysical truths of things are regarded as more mysterious while also more real than sensory perceptions and mental concepts; also used as a title for an esoteric rite or ritual intended to stimulate interest and insight about those deeper truths.

Mystic Tie: ordinarily refers to the mysterious bond that Masons feel with each other; in a mystical sense, it is the universal interconnectedness of things and between them and That which is their transcendent source.

Noesis: direct intuition; noted in Chapter 3 as the function enabling perception of the Form of the Good and the other archetypes that give rise to everything in the Visible Realm.

Oneness: a state or condition of unity, whether in the singularity of something, the communion of two or more things, or the interconnectedness of parts that form one thing; mystically speaking, it is understood to be the fundamental truth of reality, where That may thus be referred to as the ever-present, all-encompassing, all-pervading One of which each thing is a limited yet interconnected expression.

Otherness: a condition of distinction between things; in mysticism, it refers to the basic duality required for manifestation of all the diversity in existence, a necessary condition for the One's self-expressions in space and time; it does not require a destruction or denial of oneness, yet the illusion of separation results from a kind of intoxication with the otherness of oneself.

Prayer: from a mystical perspective, any act of intentionally trying to commune with That which is regarded as most sacred, true, or real; in various spiritualities, prayer may also be directed to spiritual beings like those of a pantheon, an angelic hierarchy, or to saints, ancestors, or nature spirits.

Realization: literally "making real," refers to the process of becoming as aware as possible of something, having deeper insight and understanding about it, manifesting a potentiality, or fulfilling or accomplishing some intention or desire; mystical realization is all of these developing with regard to unity, wholeness, and harmony.

Reflection: the process of an individual or group reviewing an experience to gain greater awareness of and understanding about it; an essential contemplative practice for self-awareness and self-understanding, and a useful tool for discovering unity, wholeness, and harmony in hindsight.

Relaxation: the process of releasing tension and calming and quieting the body, emotions, and mind; an indispensable element of most contemplative practices, which commonly involves rhythmic breathing techniques and facilitates a shift toward more specific states and activities of consciousness.

Ritual: any act or series of acts regularly repeated in an established particular manner; in mysticism, ritual is used by individuals and groups to shift consciousness to stimulate greater awareness, understanding, and manifestations of unity, wholeness, and harmony, including the facilitation of resiliency in maintaining a mystical perspective; in wisdom traditions like Masonry, ritual is the central means of initiation and instruction.

Self: somewhat synonymous with *soul* or *psyche*, the unique fluid network of a multitude of physical, emotional, intellectual, social, and spiritual factors that comprise the whole of an individual being, much of it outside of personal awareness; from a mystical perspective, while much of the self is changing and temporary, its mysterious essence, often referred to as *spirit*, is eternally one with That which is regarded as most sacred, true, or real; each self is regarded as a limited expression of That; spelled with a capital S, it represents That as the Transcendent, Divine, or Cosmic Self.

Self-Image: discussed extensively in Chapters 2 through 4, a mental representation of the self, or who and what one believes one is; because we lack complete awareness of the self and are subject to things like cultural conditioning and unconscious hopes and fears, the self-image is always incomplete and distorted; a major development in self-knowledge is realizing that the self-image is not the self but a mask on it.

Shadow: a largely hidden aspect of self that is developed through the processes of repression, suppression, and denial, essentially everything within the self that has been rejected by external conditioning and the ego in the process of developing the self-image; such things can emerge and express themselves with little awareness and control and thus in very harmful ways; *Shadow work* is the contemplative process of self-inquiry that attempts to bring the contents of the Shadow to personal awareness and integrate them for greater psychospiritual wholeness and harmony.

Spiritual Glamor: introduced in the Preface, the perception or belief that spirituality is, or should always be, a dramatic, exciting, or entertaining experience, which is typically motivated by escapist and self-aggrandizing desires; a major illusion that can foster instability, fragmentation, and disharmony in the self, especially conflict between the self-image and the Shadow, and contributes to shallowness and inconsistency in spiritual pursuits.

Toleration: the practice of not actively disregarding, opposing, resisting, or excluding people because of differing opinions, beliefs, or practices; discussed in Chapter 5 as the virtue that is the most basic expression of Masonry's Principal Tenets – Brotherly Love, Relief, and Truth.

Transformation: a significant change in structure or composition; for mystics, it is the refinement and reorganization of the various elements of the self, and thus the self-image, toward greater unity, wholeness, and harmony within itself as well as with others and That which is regarded as most sacred, true, or real.

Transcendent: a quality or condition beyond ordinary limits; mystically speaking, it is a state of consciousness unrestricted by thoughts and feelings, yet inclusive of all that can be experienced and known; also refers to the incomprehensibleness, ineffableness, and un-manifestness of That which is regarded as most sacred, true, or real.

Unconscious: a state or quality of unawareness; in the field of depth psychology, terms like *subconscious* and *unconscious* refer to parts of the self that typically are not directly accessible to personal awareness.

Understanding: intellectual comprehension; listed in Chapter 2 as the second of a cyclical three-step pattern experienced on contemplative paths, in which one develops more valid and reliable concepts about one's experiences and how to manifest one's intentions.

Unity: oneness; in mysticism, terms like *unitive experience* refer to special events of transcendence that impart directly intuited knowledge of union with That which is regarded as most sacred, true, or real.

Virtue: a way of morally excellent thinking and behaving that is developed through deliberate consideration and habituation; every virtue is understood as manifesting on a continuum between the extremes of excess and lack, with the classic example being that the virtue of fortitude or courage is in the middle ground between the excess of rashness and the lack that is cowardice.

Visible Realm: presented in Chapter 3 as the lower levels of Plato's Divided Line, where consciousness is characterized by enmeshment in the physical senses and dominated by consensus views, common sense, illusions, and conjectures.

Wholeness: a state of complete integration among distinct yet complementary parts; as noted in Chapter 2, it has a functional dimension such that things are more than the sum of their parts when those parts are brought together in harmony; mystics aim to more fully realize wholeness in themselves and in communion with other beings and That which is regarded as most sacred, true, or real.

Wisdom: commonly, the ability to effectively apply insight, experience, and understanding; mystically speaking, an aspect of the Divine reflected in human beings by the integration of reverent respect for life's mysteries with intuition, inspiration, ordinary mental processes, emotion, and action, which facilitates greater realization of unity, wholeness, and harmony for oneself and others.

RECOMMENDED READING

Bogdan, H. (2007). *Western Esotericism and Rituals of Initiation*. State University of New York.

Bradshaw, S., & Wallace, B. (2021). *A Path to Providence: The Creation of the Middle Chamber Program*. Laudable Pursuit.

Buck, R. (2020). *Cosmic Consciousness: A Study in the Evolution of the Human Mind*. Walking Lion.

Carmody, D., & Carmody, J. (1996). *Mysticism: Holiness East and West*. Oxford University.

Churton, T. (2009). *Freemasonry: The Reality*. Lewis Masonic.

Davis, R. (2021). *In Search of Light: A Course of Hieroglyphic and Moral Instruction for the Symbolic Lodge*. Building Stone.

Dunning, C. (2016). *Contemplative Masonry: Basic Applications of Mindfulness, Meditation, and Imagery for the Craft*. Stone Guild.

— (2021). *The Contemplative Lodge: A Manual for Masons Doing Inner Work Together*. Stone Guild.

— (2023). *A Rose Croix Oratory: Rosicrucian Reflections and Resources from a Knight of the Eagle and Pelican*. Stone Guild.

Ellwood, R. (2012). *Mysticism and Religion*. Seven Bridges.

Forman, R. (1997). *The Problem of Pure Consciousness*. Oxford University.

— (1998). *The Innate Capacity: Mysticism, Psychology, and Philosophy*. Oxford University.

— (1999). *Mysticism, Mind, Consciousness*. State University of New York.

Harvey, A. (1997). *The Essential Mystics: Selections from the World's Great Wisdom Traditions*. Harpers.

Johnson, R. (2013). *Owning Your Own Shadow: Understanding the Dark Side of the Psyche*. Harper Collins.

Komjathy, L. (2015). *Contemplative Literature*. State University of New York.

— (2018). *Introducing Contemplative Studies*. Wiley Blackwell.

Lamb, J. (2020). *Approaching the Middle Chamber: The Seven Liberal Arts in Freemasonry & the Western Esoteric Tradition*. Laudable Pursuit.

— (2021). *The Archetypal Temple, and Other Writings on Masonic Esotericism*. Lulu.com

MacNulty, W. (1991). *Freemasonry: A Journey Through Ritual and Symbol*. Thames and Hudson.

— (2006). *Freemasonry: Symbols, Secrets, Significance*. Thames and Hudson.

— (2017). *The Way of the Craftsman: A Search for the Spiritual Essence of Craft Freemasonry, Deluxe Edition*. Plumbstone.

— (2018). *Contemplating Craft Freemasonry*. Plumbstone.

Plante, T. (2010). *Contemplative Practices in Action: Spirituality, Meditation, and Health*. Praeger.

Sachs, R. (2016). *The Ecology of Oneness: Awakening in a Free World*. iUniverse.

Schuchard, M. (2002). *Restoring the Temple of Vision: Cabalistic Freemasonry and Stuart Culture*. Brill.

Sickels, D. (1871). *The General Ahiman Rezon and Freemason's Guide*. New York Masonic.

Stace, W. (1989). *Mysticism and Philosophy*. London Macmillan.

Stavish, M. (2021). *The Path of Freemasonry: The Craft as Spiritual Practice*. Inner Traditions.

Venzi, F. (2016). *Freemasonry: The Esoteric Tradition*. Lewis Masonic.

Versluis, A. (2007). *Magic and Mysticism: An Introduction to Western Esotericism*. Rowman & Littlefield.

— (2015). *Perennial Philosophy*. New Cultures.

— (2017). *Platonic Mysticism: Contemplative Science, Philosophy, Literature, and Art*. State University of New York.

Wilmshurst, W. (2007). *The Meaning of Masonry, Revised Edition*. Plumbstone.

— (2007). *The Masonic Initiation, Revised Edition*. Plumbstone.

Zaehner, R. (1980). *Mysticism, Sacred and Profane: An Inquiry into Some Varieties of Praeternatural Experience*. Oxford University.

Zajonc, A. (2009). *Meditation as Contemplative Inquiry: When Knowing Becomes Love*. Lindisfarne.

Zweig, C., & Abrams, J. (1991). *Meeting the Shadow: The Hidden Power of the Dark Side of Human Nature*. J.P. Tarcher.

ABOUT THE AUTHOR

C.R. "Chuck" Dunning, Jr. is a contemplative author, advocate, consultant, and facilitator. He has over 35 years of experience in mysticism and esotericism, as well as a career in mental health and higher education. His special interests are in traditions like Freemasonry, Rosicrucianism, and esoteric Christianity. Chuck is a Thirty-Third Degree Scottish Rite Mason, a co-founder and trainer in the Masonic Legacy Society, a Full Member of both the Texas Lodge of Research and Oklahoma Lodge of Research, and a lineage holder in two different Rosicrucian systems. His other books include *A Rose Croix Oratory: Rosicrucian Reflections and Resources from a Knight of the Eagle and Pelican* (2023), *The Contemplative Lodge: A Manual for Masons Doing Inner Work Together* (2021), and *Contemplative*

Masonry: Basic Applications of Mindfulness, Meditation, and Imagery for the Craft (2016). Chuck was also a contributing author for *The Art and Science of Initiation* (2019). In 2018, the readers of *Fraternal Review* ranked him among the top ten esoteric Masonic authors, and in 2021 they chose *Contemplative Masonry* as third among the top Masonic books since the turn of the millennium. Chuck is a facilitator of customized workshops and retreats and is a popular guest speaker for both in-person and virtual events. His work can be followed through the Contemplative Builder YouTube Channel, the Contemplative Builder Facebook page, and ChuckDunning.com.

Made in the USA
Columbia, SC
20 November 2024

46984392R00143